Pretty BROKEN

Transforming Scars to Beauty Marks

COMPILED BY NATIMA SHEREE

Published by: Words Matter, Co.

ISBN: 9798706556211

Printed in the United States of America

First Edition

TABLE OF CONTENTS

DEDICATION

This book is dedicated to our younger selves…

the young ladies who worked their asses off to become

the *Pretty* Dope women we are today.

Pretty Deep Wounds

Alyse Carter

I share with you a segment of my life that so many young women face in today's society. It's when we tend to lower our standards and try to find the good in others. However, sometimes it's not our place to find the good in others. Sometimes we're warned to run away and never look back. What do you do when you've been given clear instructions that can save your life, but it's uncomfortable?

I can literally recall the day that I sacrificed my spiritual walk for a guy that one day broke my heart into pieces, and continued to break it until I got the strength to see my own worth. I share with you this testimony to inspire you to be patient, be observant, and most importantly listen to that quiet voice that comes to warn us. This voice is sometimes so faint and so quiet, but the message it brings holds much weight and can often redirect the course of our life if we're not obedient to it. Some categorize this voice as our intuition, our gut feelings, our ancestors, The Universe, but for me I know it was the Holy Spirit that I foolishly ignored.

Before I get started, my disclaimer is that I'm no saint. I am a young black woman from urban America, whose walk is not very different from what others face. My only defense mechanism is my ability to be optimistic in midst of pure turmoil, and a constant renewing of my mind. I've had to push through many growing pains. Whether that's mentally, physically, or emotionally as a single mother but also as a former domestic abuse victim. I've also had to grow spiritually in the same world full of temptations, distractions, and intense peer pressure from everywhere. With that being said, I can practically pinpoint the biggest regret of my entire life, and I don't have many. I wish I could say I didn't see the red-flags to the greatest warning of my life, but they were there hidden in plain sight. That regret was compromising my spiritual walk with God for a temporary relationship with a man.

I was a few months short of turning 21 years old. I was attending my local junior college because my high school seemed to screw up ACT/SAT scores and going off to college had to be put on hold. Besides, my mom was unwilling to compromise anything I needed to leave. During those times, our relationship was very rocky. I felt as if my mom was sabotaging my chances of going off to college. To this day I still can't understand why I couldn't get her support, but I remembered hating her for it. I resented all the advice she would give me, and I turned to my friends and drugs for comfort. Then my world got even more chaotic when she allowed my brother and his entire family to move in. Our house felt like that movie, Hotel Transylvania. We had every type of personality in our home, and privacy was non-existent. We went from 6 people to an overwhelming 12 people in a three-bedroom house. I was desperate for a break and just wanted to run away. I wanted to disown my family, start a new life, and stay gone. This living arrangement lasted for over 8 months, and emotionally I was going through it.

One day my friend invited me over to this random guy's house to sit with her as she braided his hair. I didn't want to go at all, but I could tell in her voice that she needed someone there for her to feel safe. So I dragged myself out of the house to meet her. Well it was obvious I didn't want to be there, and I was for sure not that fun and bubbly friend that day. After sitting in complete irritation, two of this guy's neighbors walked in and I have to admit they were fine. One was brown skin, really quiet, and had a serious athletic physique. The second guy wasn't as athletic but his personality for sure stood out. He stood about

6'5, light skin, about 300 lbs, and had a head full of gorgeous curls. The moment he saw me he instantly tried to cheer me up with his sarcastic but flirtatious insults.

Throwing out cute but insulting comments, I finally gave in and lightened up. We later exchanged numbers, and long story short he didn't call me for at least 3 weeks in a row. My pride was challenged, and I was so confused. Although it was difficult to accept I felt led on. Eventually, I got fed up, called him up angrily; asking why he didn't call me! At that time, I, unfortunately, didn't take that as a sign that he wasn't all that interested in me. I didn't see that the lack of attention was a sign that he just wasn't the guy for me. I challenged him just like the first day we met. My pride was hurt, and I wasn't used to being ignored. I mean I grew up with four big brothers, and attention was the last thing I had to demand. He simply apologized and informed me that his house was under construction, and it was occupying a majority of his time.

Our first couple of dates were equivalent to storybook dates. He would pick me up with flowers, open the door, we laughed good, and ate even better. I was barely 21 and was being introduced to some of the best steakhouses Chicago could offer. This guy was showing me a whole new world.

When my birthday rolled around I got treated like a queen. I mean he went totally out of the way for my birthday, and we've only known each other for about a month. I was given a Pandora bracelet, a couple of outfits from the mall, an amazing skyline dinner, and the next couple of days we just clubbed our hearts out. He was a confident dancer that demanded the room's attention, and all drinks were on him. I was in complete party bliss as a new 21-year-old, especially knowing I was so unhappy with my lifestyle back at my parents. I found too much comfort in this new guy.

We formed the habit of calling each other daily, and he would rescue me whenever I called. Later on, I realized I shouldn't have told him just how uncomfortable I was at home, because then he soon started inviting me back to his house. Of course, that wasn't the first invite, especially after these romantic dinners, but I wanted to keep this guy waiting. I needed him to respect me for my boundaries. Besides, I only had 2 sexual partners before getting to know him. So we went out on numerous dates before I finally accepted his offer to go back to his house.

The first time I visited this guy's house, it completely reeked of urine and I could barely breathe. I instantly got a headache and was kind of embarrassed for him. There were beer cans and old pizza boxes everywhere. The kitchen floor was Grimmy with visible dirt, and the trash was filled to the top. Upstairs the maintenance of the bathroom held no feminine touch, and on his bedroom door hung a fraternity paddle. The second bedroom had blood stains all over the walls. I couldn't help but to hold my nose, and observe everything during this initial walkthrough. The upkeep of the house simply didn't match who this guy was showing me. He was neat, smelt amazing, great job, foreign car, but lived in a complete shack.

He tried explaining to me that he recently had a total of 3 Pitbulls, and was forced to get rid of the males because of the constant dog-fighting which explained the blood, but the fact the dogs busted through his large front living room window. They were out of control, and the upkeep of his place was horrendous. During that time, I was so thirsty to stay away from my home that I tried to also justify why his place looked so horrible. I ignored the infamous quote I personally practiced which was, Cleanliness is next to Godliness. Everything was trashed. One day his father visited us and made the comment to me. I don't know how someone so pretty and put together can tolerate the smell of this place, let alone accept someone so dirty. I was embarrassed for this guy on how rude and direct his father was, but I had a choice to make.

I didn't want to challenge his ego or call out the obvious. So I ignored everything that bothered me. Besides, I didn't want to be at my house anyway, and maybe he just needed a little help around his house.

I tried to convince myself so many times why this man's behavior didn't match the lifestyle that was behind closed doors. So I bit my tongue about the nature of the house. I rolled up my sleeves as most females do, I started showing that I could be a good woman, by cooking and cleaning. I thought I could change him by showing off some of my life skills. Boy was I wrong!

This man stood before me so proud to be a town-house owner at 25 with a flourishing career. Ignoring the nature of his house, or that he was always late to work. The vision he had for his future and his future family. I wanted to fit in with the idea of being the wife of a future politician. Although at the time, he didn't have any requisite to support his dream, yet. He spoke of so many great things and wanting to see the world. You could see the love and pride in his eyes as he dreamed aloud. How this man talked and described everything he wanted out of life; he was selling me a dream and I was buying it. Although, the smell of the house resembled hell or at least a dirty subway station.

I figured, he came from successful parents so that was even more reason to believe him. His mother was an entrepreneur and his father was the Vice President of some huge technology company. Although his parents were divorced by the time he was 10, I only saw the positive. Ignoring the fact that as an early psychology student that i should have made an impact on his life at such an impressionable age. Later on, I found out that it did when issues would arise, and how he would respond to me. My eyes were wide shut. His mother embraced me with open arms, and his dad adored me, even thanked me once for being with his son. Never did I take that as a sign, because it fed my ego that I was valued in this man's family.

Until, one day I was spending the night over his house as usual by this time, and he asked me a question that made me totally uncomfortable. By this time we've had sex a few times but always protected, until he asked to take the condom off. Initially, I was completely turned off. This guy was 5 years older, in a fraternity, and was obviously a lot more experienced than me. When I say, I heard the

Holy Spirit speak to me as clear as day warning me. The message was so terrifying, but yet so quiet that I should have run out the door with my clothes in my hand to never return. The message was, "If you lay with this man unprotected you will experience years of heartache and I will not be able to save you from everything you're going to experience".

What do you do when you hear that message at 3 am and you're already in the position of being peer pressured, and the environment is set to say go??? I'll tell you what you do, YOU LEAVE! You run! You don't compromise or take a chance to test the limits! No matter how uncomfortable or what someone says, you listen to that voice. That's what you do. Never ever, put yourself second to what you know your heart feels, no matter how uncomfortable you are. I should have run in total disgust. And guess what, that small voice that came at 3 am was right.

Three months later I went in for a regular check-up to find out I was now 21 years old and pregnant but that wasn't the worst part. When the nurse practitioner gave me my bloodwork results back, I instantly started to throw up in the middle of her office. Not only did I find out I was pregnant but this man gave me an STI. I felt as if my life was ruined, never had I experienced something as discomforting as receiving this news until I told him and I was even more disgusted. As we sat in front of the local corner-store, I told him in the car that I was pregnant and my bloodwork results, and his response was, "at least we don't have to wear protection going forward". I could have burned him alive with all the anger that raged from just my eyes alone. It was so far from what I expected that I felt as if he knew the entire time and intentionally plotted against me. I felt as if this was a trap to keep me close to him. I felt the ultimate betrayal, my heart sunk deep into the pit of my belly.

I fell into a deep depression, I couldn't eat, I was losing weight fast, and I was far from myself. I stopped dressing up and being optimistic was the last thing I wanted to be. It came to a point where I was standing in front of the mirror crying, not even recognizing my own face. I turned away from everyone, even ran away from my relationship with God out of embarrassment, because I recalled the warning over my life and I foolishly ignored Him. I didn't think things could get any worse, I mean this guy was still standing by my side.

Well, five months into my pregnancy the truth about this guy was starting to surface up quickly. I started noticing a drinking problem, and his sarcastic comments started becoming straight out disrespectful insults. Whenever I bring up any future plans about this child, I would get a serious pushback. Financial challenges started to expose this man's priorities. He would buy cases of beer and alcohol daily, eating out often, but the lights were cut off. When we got the light bill under control, then the water would get shut off. Once we finally got out of the hole with my planning, he then would want to spend every extra penny on going out and partying. By that time and due to my pregnancy, partying was the last thing I wanted. I needed to prepare. I needed to prepare financially, keeping my savings in total secrecy.

I was in over my head with this relationship, but I felt as if I was in too deep. This man would often tell me that no one wanted me, and my family didn't want me back home either. He was going to be the only man that would love me through everything we just experienced in the last six months. He was now the complete opposite of the gentleman that he initially advertised. Then things got even worst. Whenever he would get drunk and his friends would make a comment about my beauty or anything positive associated with me, he wouldn't address it directly with them. Instead, at the end of the night, he would start a fight with me that resulted on many occasions him choking me or hemming me to the wall. I wanted to literally kill myself for all that I've allowed, and I attempted to do just that.

On my 22nd birthday, I was big and pregnant and none of my family knew the turmoil I was facing. The family house is still more crowded than ever. There was no privacy anywhere and my bedroom was taken over. I sat on the bathroom floor with the shower running, hysterically crying in silence. I've had enough. It was too much to bear and I just wanted to end it all. I could literally visualize myself slitting my wrist and seeing my family's reaction as they found my lifeless body. These images replayed in my head over and over again. Until I gained the courage to pick myself off the bathroom floor and turned back to God. I begged God for an escape because I knew I could never see better days if I ended my life right here, but the emotional pain cut so deep. The fact no one knew the pain I was experiencing is what cut even deeper, but God knew my pain, and he tried to warn me too. I cannot deny the Holy Spirit tried to give me an exit before it even started, and I denied Him, and that was the biggest regret I can say I hold to this day.

Now I stand tall and firm and absolutely confident in the woman I am today. I am proud of myself, but the damage that was caused in an 18-month abusive relationship literally took me years to rebuild. I had to first and foremost turn back to God. I apologized and repented for not trusting in Him and the warning from the Holy Spirit. I had to make an oath to myself to never compromise what I know is right spiritually for temporary gratification. On several occasions, I've had to isolate myself, seek counseling, pray, and fast for a clean and bitter-free heart. I had to learn how to not hate someone who tried to destroy me, spread rumors about me, to then turn around and play a victim for sympathy.

If it had not been for the greatest gift of the Holy Spirit, I don't know where I would be. So I leave with you the words and the scriptures that literally saved my life when I wanted to give up.

Joshua 10:25 - Do not be afraid or dismayed; be strong and courageous. For thus the Lord will do to all your enemies against whom you fight. AND Deuteronomy 31:6 - Be strong and courageous. Do not fear or be in dread of them, for it is the Lord your God who goes with you. He will never leave you nor forsake you.

If you don't consider yourself religious or you've been hurt or judged by those who claim to have a faith walk. I challenge you to challenge God to show Himself to you, so you may gain further confidence and knowledge in Him. We are and will forever be in challenging times, and if you can understand that a majority of issues we face are first spiritual that manifests itself physically, then you can gain the power to change your world and everyone around you.

I walk in peace, love, and understanding for all those who are for me and extended blessings towards those who are against me. As they do not fully understand the control the enemy still has over them, and require even more patience, and understanding from those who are spiritually mature and in power.

Pretty PAINFUL

Catherine Robinson

Broken-hearted He heals the brokenhearted and binds up their wounds Psalm 147:3. Through painful circumstances, I learned the true meaning of love and sacrifice. Circumstances that broke my young heart yet healed my soul forever. The defining moment of my life was the catalyst that matured me into the woman I am today; resilient, faithful, courageous, and healed.

My story is a release of sorrow held only in my heart and re-lived in my memory. It is laying to rest one of God's most precious gifts to me. This story is dedicated to my Son and the lessons of his existence that restored my soul. Love Don't Live Here Come to me, all who are weary and burdened and I will give you rest. For my yoke is easy and my burden is light. Matthew 11:28:30. I grew up with the materialistic and social resources of a perfect home. There was nothing out of reach or anything too big for me to accomplish.

My parents ingrained the importance of education, career, and financial stability into my young mind. I watched both of my parent's dedication to providing a nice home and security for my sister and I. I felt safe and secure as any child should. On the outside looking in, we were the "Robinson's" a picture-perfect family. However, behind the solid foundation was an emotionally broken home. Warmth and love did not reside within the security of our four walls. Though we lived under one roof, distance, isolation, and a cold draft occupied the space of my home. At close distance, I watched my parents have an unloving and emotionless marriage. The spirit of love did not resonate through the hallways of our house. We all lived parallel to one another and in our own worlds. My mother was a great mother who ensured that we were protected and provided for, we had all the latest and new material things any child could ask for.

My mother was fun, she loved to cook and sew. She poured into our spirit, uplifted our self-esteem, and reiterated that we were loved. She made sure we were engaged in meaningful life activities like girls Empowerment groups and girl scouts. My father was strong, commanding, serious, and distant. I longed for his acknowledgment and affection. I wanted to be Daddy's girl. I knew in my heart that I was supposed to be Daddy's girl, but his own unresolved emotional pain prevented him from being the father he wanted to be. I needed the male reassurance and protection that only a father could provide. I held a vague feeling of rejection and unworthiness from him. I knew my father loved me, but he had a hard time expressing it. I always say that my mother has a huge heart of gold. She is patient, forgiving, and accommodating to others. She believed in her marriage, happiness, and my father whom she deeply loved. She waited patiently and I am sure prayed for his healing so that our family could thrive under proper male leadership.

At the age of six, I recognized that my family dynamic was not healthy. I would observe my environment and my feelings concerning the interactions between my parents. I either instinctively knew or God began speaking to me about his true intention for marriage and family. I knew that a family meant loving kindness and I knew I longed for my father who I deeply admired. I knew at this age that I wanted something different and better for myself. I wanted to experience the fullness of love, connection, and happiness.

My family dynamic was a secret. On the outside looking in we looked ideal. But inside our home was quietness and a subtle fear. My father's commanding energy carried a heaviness that I dare not cross or question. My natural childlike nature and longing for a loving father were silenced and I grew to take care of myself emotionally at a young age. Because of the lack of communication between my parents, I learned to keep my needs to myself as to not burden my mother. I learned to show a smiling face to the world, while I emotionally suffered in silence. The quietness of my home opened a world of daydreaming and making plans for my future. I learned to be observant, introspective, and a planner. I also took on the trait of reservation and shyness to avoid the attention that could shine a light on my family's secret. I wanted nothing more than to escape and be free, happy, and experience warmth in love and acceptance. My parents separated when I was 12. I was proud of my mother for taking such a meaningful and healing step to enrich her life. My life with my mother and sister was happy. The three of us together thrived in being open and warmth filled our new home. My father was still present in my life, but the years of his silence and the heaviness of his spirit made me unsure of how to love him.

Bruised and Battered but not broken by his stripes we are healed. Isaiah 53:5. As the new girl in 11th grade, it was easy to stick out like a sore thumb. My first day of a new High School was intimidating to say the least. I did not know anyone, and I felt alone in a room full of bright students. I felt self-conscious and out of place. All I wanted was to make a friend on the first day so that I would not have to eat lunch alone. Throughout the day, I stayed quiet trying to shrink my slim 5'7 frame as small as possible to not be noticed. As the day went on and true to my nature, I observed my environment, the teachers, the students, and began to find some comfort and friendship with a few young ladies. My first day was going well before a fateful meeting outside of the school gates. At the end of the day, He met me and not the other way around. He was attracted to me like a bee is to honey. It was as if he was a roaring lion seeking out his prey. I am certain he studied me from afar and laid in wait for the right time to approach. He carefully examined my shyness and reservations about my new school and made his plans for me in his calculated mind to use for his advantage. He was tall, charming, and assertive and made it clear that he was the only boy in school who would ever have me. He was interested in me and wanted to know who I was beyond a superficial level.

After school, he would walk me home and he would ask me questions about my life, feelings, and family. He made me feel safe, secure, and protected so I divulged all my life dreams and secrets. I told him about my childhood and the significant relationships and experiences in my life. As young "love" goes, he quickly became my first boyfriend. As quickly as the relationship began, the interaction between him and I changed too. He was older and more experienced, and he led the direction of the relationship. One day after school, he said to me "since your mother has a meeting today, come to my house instead of going home". I felt confused because I had not told him that my mother would not be home on this day. He remembered and kept note of the details of my household patterns from previous conversations. I experienced a vague feeling of apprehension and a violation of my boundaries at this moment. I knew in my heart, that I should have gone home. However, the domineering tone of his voice and the wickedness behind his eyes sent a subtle fear through my heart so I agreed to his plan.

Walking to his house, I knew what would happen. I could hear my mother's voice saying, "don't let any boys touch you and don't have sex". All that she had taught me was playing in the background of my mind as I was trying to back out of the decision to go to my boyfriend's house. I told him that I must go home right now! "If I am not home by 4:00 pm, my mother will be scared". He dismissed my protest and insisted I go with him or else he would start a rumor about me at school. As we walked, it was as if a knife had been stabbed in my back. He actively betrayed my trust and broke my confidence as he took my virginity. I felt confused and exposed. The boy who was my protector had pressured me into having sex. Verbally I had consented, but emotionally and spiritually I was robbed of my innocence which sent me into a deep state of guilt and self-isolation. His kind words and compliments turned into slurs and demeaning insults. Ugly, hideous, stupid, and phrases such as "no one likes you", "your father can't stand you " and "everyone thinks you are dumb" were the sentiments of our conversations. All the emotions and feelings that I had confided in him, he had used against me. As the weeks went on, he began to threaten me with physical assaults if I did not go home with him after school. I felt that I had no one to turn to. As my fear of him grew, I mustered up the courage to tell him "NO MORE". This was the first day he slapped me clear across my face just out of sight from the crowd of students. The painful sting broke my spirit and yet I managed to smile as I greeted my teacher that morning. That first slap turned into choking, arm grabbing, pushing, and fingers in my face, if I disagreed with him or displayed any sense of individual strength. I could not believe the hole I had dug for myself or the betrayal of someone who I trusted. My once sunny demeanor carried a gray cloud of sadness. I was trapped, bruised, and broken and I had no way to escape. No One Saw Me You saw me before I was born. Every day of my life was recorded in your book psalms

139:16. The weeks of verbal abuse and threats seemed like years. I began to shut down as he isolated me and blocked me from forming friendships. My new school was supposed to be a new beginning, yet it turned into a living nightmare in which I was the main character, yet I was invisible. I covered the bruises from his abuse, and I replaced it with a smile to hide the pain and fear I held inside. My relationship with my boyfriend moved so quickly, that I did not have any support from friends to stand up to him. Besides, I had already been betrayed by someone who I confided in; I did not trust anyone, and I was alone. Because of fear, I was forced into lies to my mother and the whole of my despair grew deeper. The guilt and shame overtook me. I felt like a sheep in a valley of wolves, with no protection from the person who intentionally hurt me the most. The trust of life I once had abandoned me, but I still knew something greater was intended for me. So, I began praying and asked the Lord to save me, protect me and love me back to life. Although no evident at the time. The Lord my God keep his promise.

A female's intuition is powerful, the moment the baby was conceived I felt it. I knew it in my soul, I instantly changed. There was a presence and peace about this little life growing rapidly. My boyfriend had gained so much control over me and studied me so well, he knew I was pregnant before I told him. He was ecstatic with joy at the thought of becoming a father at just 17 years old. On the other hand, I was devasted and confused at the thought of being a mother at 16. My life flashed before my eyes. How was I going to have a baby while in High School, go to college and live the dream my parents planned for me with a verbally and physically abusive man. I could not fathom the pain that I had already experienced for the rest of my life. I felt ruined, sick, and in despair. The whole experience was so deep, I could not tell my mother. I did not want to hurt her or and did not know how to explain the trauma, abuse, and coercion I had been experiencing. I felt that I would have been blamed for the entire circumstance. I already felt misunderstood by my family, so I keep my pregnancy a secret. The secret which I held so close became my peace and the most intimate experience of my life.

My thoughts and daydreams surrounded the life I carried inside of me. I hid this life under my clothes, rubbing my belly and feeling kicks and bumps as the weeks went on. I sacrificed physical and emotional pain for this blessed secret that grew inside of me. My secret became my first love, my reason for living, my joy and anticipation. At school, I would protect my growing belly with my oversized school sweater and books. I promised my baby that I would do anything to make sure it was safe and protected.

During this time, my boyfriend softened his approach to me. The physical abuse stopped, but the verbal abuse continued. The highs and lows of the pregnancy put me on a one passenger roller coaster ride. I was suffering in silence and keeping secrets all the while trying to sustain life. I had prayed and begged God to save me. I could not believe God allowed me to experience betrayal, abuse, and top it off with a pregnancy. How did I allow this to happen? Why didn't God intervene? How did I end up in an abusive relationship as a teenager? I cried out to God, I was angry, yet thankful that he sent me a reminder of his blessing and sovereignty. Nevertheless, I was conflicted. Was I ready to live a life of ongoing pain? Trapped Who the Son sets Free, is Free Indeed. John 8:36. Finally, I felt freedom. My growing belly and chubby face finally could not be hidden any longer. My mother asked the inevitable question "Catherine, are you pregnant?" My secret was exposed. It was a relief to not hide any longer and for my mother to help manage my health and be a barrier between me and the source of my fear. Instead of relief, I was met with persecution which I feared all along. Instead of asking questions or hearing my experience, it was assumed I wanted the pregnancy to happen. It was assumed that I was out living my life and enjoying a grown relationship with my boyfriend. In actuality, I was in bondage and my young mind and reasoning did not know how to escape. I was speechless and could not form the words to explain my ordeal. How could I explain that I had been threatened, taunted, and physically abused while in the relationship with my boyfriend?.

Fear and trauma had me once again feeling abandoned and misunderstood. My experience was out in the open airing out like dirty laundry. However, the vilest part of my experience was still held inside of my memory with bruises to prove it. I was pressured to give myself away, beaten down body and spirit. Freedom was snatched from my peace and I was trapped by the judgment and perception of the world around me. The visit to the Obstetrician /Gynecologist showed that I was about 23 weeks pregnant and entering my 6th month. During the sonogram, the nurse said, "would you like to see your son?". I experienced joy once again and the sudden knowing this baby is real.

I had a new secret; I only knew I was to be the mother of a son. The drive home with my mother was silent, but I was carried away in my daydreams thinking about the life to come. After all that I had been through in such a short period of time, there was a joy at the end of this tunnel. My son was to be my purpose in life, the first real love I would experience. I was going to protect him at all cost. Later in the week my mother and my boyfriend's mother asked me "well when do you plan to have an abortion". My heart dropped. I could not believe the words I was hearing. I understood their grief and disappointment, but I expected their compassion and protection. The one promise I made to my baby lay in the balance. How could they not see an obviously pregnant girl sitting on the sofa across from them? The mention of death consumed me, and I cried myself to sleep and held my belly tight that night. In my heart, I knew these would be the last few days of his life. For three nights, my mother and my boyfriends' mother talked at me providing reasons to support abortion. The reasons mainly being that I am ruining my future and the perception of the world and my extended family would have on me.

For two of the three nights of intense pressure to abort my son, I stood firm and refused. My boyfriend's mother was a nurse, she knew timelines for abortion like the back of her hand. Within 7 days it would be too late to abort my son. Therefore, persuasion and pressure were time-sensitive to ensure that my sons' life did not disrupt theirs. Going on 6 months pregnant the idea of abortion was unfathomable. I was a proponent of adoption. At least my son would have a good home with loving parents who are ready for a child. That idea was dismissed in thinking that I would grow attached and change my mind later to keep my son. From the time I spent with my son, he was very much real and alive to me. I experienced him from the very beginning, intense morning sickness, the first flutters to watching my body transform from slim to a perfectly round belly. The idea of aborting him made me sick to my soul. By the third night of pressuring at almost midnight, with a heavy dead soul, I reluctantly agreed. My mother and my boyfriends' mother were relieved. I was sick.

In the state of Maryland, abortions at 23 weeks are illegal and only should be considered if the fetus has a terminal deformity. My son was perfectly healthy and strong. My boyfriends' mother had already researched and had lists of facilities and hospitals that perform abortions at this stage. On that very night at 12:32 am, I was told to pack an overnight bag quickly because we needed to go to New York City. "Blessed are those who mourn, for they will be comforted" Matthew 5:4. I could not believe what was happening to me. During the drive to New York in the midnight hours, I felt numb. I was not seen, not heard, not considered. I felt like an utter disgrace and no one asked how I was feeling emotionally. It was as if this choice of life was not my own. I understood and respected my mother's feelings and beliefs about teenage parenthood. I knew that she wanted only the best life for me. I understood her sentiment of what others would think of me and her. However, what I knew and believed to be true about myself did not matter.

After all that I had been through, in a matter of months of starting a new school, falling into a manipulative, verbally and physically abusive relationship and ultimately giving myself away out of fear, I still believed and knew that God had great plans for me. I held the things my parents engrained in me. I knew that the sky was the limit, that I would be successful in all things that I touched. I believed and knew I was blessed, and I had God's favor despite of my circumstances. I knew this event was not in vain and that it would be a testimony. This defining time of my life is when I knew God loves me the most. The greatest love of all. I held all my energy inside during that drive to New York. Anger, rage, hurt sadness, and betrayal. I wanted to scream at my boyfriend's mother because she had no idea what her son had done. She did not know how he bruised me inside and out. All of this I keep inside. I decided that mentioning this would be fruitless. In due time, she would know. I decided to focus my attention during that drive on praying and hearing from God on what was his ultimate plan for my life was. I knew then that I wanted to be a voice for teenagers, those who felt unheard, misunderstood, and unloved. Little did I know this experience was the catalyst that propelled me to study Psychology as an undergraduate and earn a master's degree in School Guidance Counseling. God was already using me, a girl who came from a "picture perfect" home, who found herself abused, unheard and unseen to be an example of faith in trusting God has an ultimate plan to bring him glory. For that, I am forever humbled and grateful. God knew I could bear this burden, and he equipped me with emotional strength to endure it. The waiting room of the abortion clinic was surreal.

Twenty years later I can recall every detail, the chairs, the smell, the magazines, and the music playing in the background. This picture in my mind will forever be in my heart because it was the last time, I felt my son, the last moments of his life. Shania Twain "From This Moment on" played. The lyrics to the song gave me closure and spoke to my soul. " Through weakness and strength, happiness and sorrow, for better, for worse, I will love you with every beat of my heart, and for your love, I'd give my last breath" Those lyrics serve as my tribute to him. When I woke up from the procedure to take my son's life, emptiness surrounded me. I wanted to cry, but I had to smile through it. I closed my eyes and shed one tear.

At that moment God promised me that I would be healed, I believed that promise and God showed himself faithful. "Blessed is she who believes that the Lord will fulfill his promise to her" Luke 1:45. This has been my power verse and a statement of my faith. My ordeal was all over. My boyfriend was a graduating senior and I took the remainder of the school year off to heal. My mother made sure I never saw my boyfriend again which was the highlight of the experience. My son was gone, and the story of this experience was wiped away. It was never spoken of again. My experience was buried, but my son lived on in my heart and in my memory.

I promised myself that I would exceed expectations of the mind, body, spirit, and soul. Testimony of faith praises you because "I am fearfully and wonderfully made " psalm 139:14. To my sorrow, God gave me beauty for his ashes, the oil of joy for mourning, and a garment of praise for the spirit of heaviness I carried with me. He forgave me for my transgressions so that I could extend forgiveness to those who crushed my spirit. Forgiveness set me free so that I could move forward towards God's plans.

My experience had the potential to either make me or break me. I choose the high road. Due to the high expectations set by my parents, the prayers over my life, and God making his presence known to me at 6 years old, I had a trust in life that transcended any pain and burdens. God who knew me before I was born, planned greater, and made me uncomfortable with the idea of settling on a life he did intend. He pushed me toward his will to further his plan for my life to be of great blessings to others. God spoke to my spirit, agitated my soul, made me restless, and gave me comfort with being set apart even in pain. Until now, my experience has been a secret, swept under the rug to prevent shame and judgment from being cast upon me and my family. God did not intend for us to hide and tremble from the judgment of this world. He is the only judge of character and Soul.

Forgiveness is a power that God offers us all. It transforms anger and hurt into healing and peace. It is a place of strength that speaks volumes about your character, mind, and soul. It not only releases the transgressor from contempt, but it opens the door of your life to be lived more abundantly. I turned over the hurt and rejection I felt from my father to God. I have an overflow of love for him that is indescribable. God allowed me, the one who felt unloved to pour God's love into him. The return of favor is that I can love others freely while meeting them where they are on their life journey.

My experience with domestic violence provided me with compassion for those who feel hard-pressed on every side with no escape. Though my high school boyfriend abused me, his influence strengthened my faith in life, and together we created God's love for us. Extending forgiveness to him allows me to release him into God's hands. Though the experience was painful, my son's life healed my soul. A mother's love is the ultimate sacrifice. It is like nothing else in the world. It knows no law, no pity, it dares all things and crushes down remorselessly all that stands in its path. A mother's love knows no bounds and will do whatever is best for her child. My mother is the most beautiful, outstanding woman I know. I hope to emulate her qualities of goodness when I become a wife. Already as a mother, I model my mother's influence by pouring confidence and love into my daughters' life. I echo the sentiments taught to me that she is valuable and worthy of all good things. I understand my mother wanted only the best for me. God knew the day that I was born the experiences I would have; it was all according to his plan. For that, we are set free from guilt and we know that God loves us and forgives us more than we could imagine. "I will restore you to health and heal your wounds declares Lord" Jeremiah 30:17. I was the keeper of secrets because no one heard me, and no one saw me. I was the keeper of my fears, the keeper of my joys and success, and the keeper of my dreams. But now I have given all my secret sorrow and the desires of my heart to God. I know that he alone is the worker of life and he hears my prayers. I know that I am set free because when God sets us free, we are free indeed. I am set free to share my journey and not be ashamed.

My truth demonstrates God's sovereignty and pulled me closer to him for protection, love, and forgiveness. Be not ashamed of your journey for it is God's Will to speak through our life circumstances to bless others. I am a survivor of teenage domestic violence, an advocate for young women and I am healed from the experience of late-term abortion. I am the mother of a 20-year-old son, whom God used to heal my soul and to give God glory. Not a day goes by that my son's memory reminds me of God's purpose for me. His life was not in vain. I lay him to rest properly, acknowledging his life as he was my love and my peace during my storm.

Pretty IS JUST A PORTION

Colleen Nero

In the Beginning

I grew up in the St. Albans section of Queens, NY.

On a quiet tree-lined street to a Southern American Mother and Trinidadian Father where the importance of God and education were paramount. My brother, who is 3 years younger and i never wanted for anything but at the same time were taught that everything is earned. We were opposites in a good I believe.

My brother was the "good kid", always followed the rules, and never wanted to get into trouble. I, on the other hand i liked to "shake the table" so to speak. I'm still reminded of that 3-year-old who decided to sit on the roof of her childhood home by kicking in the screen of the second-story bedroom window. Never a dull moment when I was around. My parents were married until I was 20 years old. They did what they could to remain happy with each other. Not to say there wasn't any arguing but they tried. My brother and I were smart, Brave, and honestly fed up to the point that we requested they divorce. Until this day I'm a little resentful towards them both for not creating an environment "enveloped in Black love", but at the end of the day, undeniably loved us very much. The relationship between my mother and father prepared me for the Rollercoaster of Love and life that I was about to experience…Or so I thought.

I took the "L" when it came to my Heart

I met "L" at a club in The Bronx in the Spring of 2004.

He was everything I wouldn't date...Tons of tattoos, braids, and shit, someone I met in The Bronx. His approach, that didn't match his outer appearance is what made me stop. It didn't match the alcohol-soaked couches and loud atmosphere engulfed with explicit music. He was Fine in the face. Medium complexion, Puerto Rican with a great smile. We talked for the remainder of the night. I was completely sprung. The next day, he called me first thing in the morning. I was so relieved that I wasn't the only one wishing that it was morning so that I could hear from him. We talked for a week before we made it "official". He was attentive, funny, smart. We were inseparable. Even though he lived in New Jersey and I lived in Queens, we made it work. He was always there no matter what.

Year 2 with "L" is when things started to go south. I would be a good Girlfriend, cook and clean his place when need be. I would find alcohol bottles here and there but it wasn't anything alarming. One night I couldn't reach him.

For 2 1/2 hours, I m thinking the worst, not that he was with another woman but that he s dead somewhere. I rode all the way to Jersey to find him in a deep comatose sleep surrounded by empty bottles of Hennessy and Vodka bottles, at the foot of the bed a puddle of vomit. I was shocked, angry, and concerned all the same time. He woke up yelling at me. Saying "Why are you here?"

"What the fuck is wrong with you?" I left crying not understanding what the hell just happened. I dodged his calls for 3 days. I needed to process what I had just witnessed and decide if it was something I could deal with being with him. I finally picked up the phone. He simply said, "I have a problem". How could I leave someone I loved and someone who was brave enough to admit I have a problem. The next week he went to Rehab upstate New York. I cried for 2 days, not only because I missed him but I wasn't used to this. Rehab and alcoholism, It was foreign to me. But I know that he was who I loved and I had to be his ride or die.

He completed a 2-month stint of rehab and it was the best thing he could have done. I felt we were renewed as a unit and separately as well. One night we decided to stay in and have date night indoors. I would cook and we would watch movies. As the night progressed, it ended in true “L” fashion, him falling asleep in my lap and I left watching the movie alone. It was all good, he worked hard. It’s 12 midnight at this point, his phone rings, I ignore it. I was never that chick to check my man’s phone. The phone rang again then again. I said maybe it s his mom or some sort of emergency. I tried to wake him up but he was like a hibernating bear. I answered and to my surprise, it was some girl on the other end. I questioned her with adrenaline pumping. The answer to the question I dreaded “Yes we had sex”. I hung up the phone and sat in a vegetated state for about 30 min. Then an estranged “Friend” made her appearance, and her name was “Rage”. I started screaming “ Wake the Fuck up!” He jumps up not knowing what day it was. I regurgitated all I was just told. I degraded him to his very core. I have never been that cruel, that angry, reckless with my mouth every. It was like Satan had taken over my body. I left. I grabbed everything that was in sight I owned and left. I went to a hotel for the night and cried. I cried for 3 hours straight. What probably hurt the most was the fact he gave himself to someone that probably wouldn’t have had the balls to stay with him when he was down and out. He gave her the glossy exterior while I had to pick up the pieces and help him through his circumstance. I refused to talk to him.

Two weeks went by when I decided to hear him out. I gave him another chance, but not for the right reasons. I didn’t trust him, but for the sake of not being alone and not giving my man to another bitch. I stayed. I carried on with the relationship as if nothing happened, but not without committing my own indiscretions.

I became a habitual cheater. It was easy and it suppressed the pain inflicted on me by "L". I was using my pretty face, My nice body as well as my anger to do what I wanted. One night I decided to take a "friend" up on his offer to have dinner. I told "L" I was having dinner with my best friend and I'll be home around 10 pm. I never made it home that night but rather 10 am the next morning. 67 missed calls and 20 voicemails. Talk about instant gratification. I had the upper hand in my eyes. I knew I was wrong but I didn't care. He was pissed and I was unbothered. It was the beginning of the end.

August 16, 2010 was the evening that changed it all. L and I went out to dinner. There was something deep down in my soul that just wasn't allowing me to have a good time. He noticed it , I was the "Non-Poker Faced Pisces". It was obvious. He asked me repeatedly what was wrong. I said I was tired and blamed it on a hectic work week. We carried on with dinner but he grew increasingly concerned yet frustrated with me. It was irritating. I was thinking to myself "Muthafucka, just eat your food so we can go". We finished dinner and walked on to the street when he approached me with question "What the fuck is wrong with you?". Now I could have said what I really wanted to say was, "I don't trust you, you re a lying alcoholic who has no idea how to please me anymore". But for the sake of the patrons eating outside, I looked at him and walked away. He grabs me by my arm and hails a taxi. I didn't make a scene by his physicality towards me because I wasn't scared. I say nothing in the cab. We were a ways away from from each of our homes so we decided to get a hotel room. We check in and I m still quiet at this point. He disappears for 1/2 hour and I didn't give a fuck! He comes back and it didn't take much to realize that he was drunk. At that point I didn't care how long it took me to get home, I wanted out of that room and him out of my sight. He grabs me by the arm and slams me against the wall. At this point I m scared because the blow was so hard I m literally seeing stars. He grabs me by the neck and punches me in the face. I m screaming at this point. He grabs me by the throat and slams me so hard up against the bathroom mirror it breaks. He stops his assault on me to throw up. That's when I ran out the room and down the stairs to the hotel lobby I m bloody with a swollen face at this point. He runs after me and continues to punch and kick me on the floor of the hotel lobby. Security jumps on him and tackles him but he somehow gets away and runs off. He was apprehended a few blocks away and placed under arrest. The police show up and the look on the officer's face said it all. I refused medical attention and I'm taken to the police station. I'm silent at this point. No crying. Nothing. It was like I was dead. I couldn't believe I was headed to the police station in the back of a squad car after having the shit beat out of me by a man I once loved. I gave my statement and had pictures taken of my swollen bloody face.

I called one of my good girlfriends to pick me up. She rushed right over to the station. That's when I broke down. The next day was the hardest. Still swollen and sore I counted 75 scratches bruises bumps etc. At the moment in time, My pretty was nonexistent. The end of this pretty amazing experience had come to an end. I walked away and never looked back.

"K" Marks the spot or did he?

Since the break up with "L", I dabbled with dating, Including one brief relationship that ended due to the fact at the beginning of the relationship, he told me he had no kids, towards the end 4 popped up. Left with the quickness and before feelings got involved. Thank you, Jesus. I turned to a popular website just for fun. I had no intentions of finding love or a boyfriend. Just a friend. I came across a profile of a man with a photo of half his face covered. Not on purpose, but it was the way the photo was captured. I was intrigued. I gathered enough courage to message him. He messaged me right away. This was new to me. I hadn't fully recovered from the trauma "L" inflicted so I wasn't expecting or wanted much. From the first conversation, I learned he was from Brooklyn and worked in a Posh Upper East Side residential building as a Doorman. We spoke for a week before he asked me out. October 24, 2014, the night of our first date. We decide to play pool. It was different yet the best first date I had ever been on.

1 week later, Halloween, our second date we made it official. Months turned into a year and it was still all good.

I thought to myself "This was it" I knew I had found my forever. There were so many things that weren't in this relationship that were in the one with "L" plus he was 8 years my senior so I had no doubt this was next level. August 8th, 2016, I was sick, sick to the point, that water made me sick. Something said take a pregnancy test… It was positive! It wasn't the right time but when is it ever the right time if it wasn't planned. He was very supportive and said it was my decision what I wanted to do. I decided not to keep it. It was a hard decision to make. The next week after the procedure, I went back to his house to rest. He ended up falling asleep next to me and 2 hours later I awoke feeling better. Still tired but confident in my decision. I felt well enough to cook dinner and do laundry. At the bottom of the hamper, was a phone. It was a burner phone that infamous "Side Chick" phone. I opened it up. Tons of text messages from different women. Telling them how beautiful they were, explicit pictures, etc. This time rage was nowhere to be found, it was complete devastation. I woke him up and the look on his face was indescribable. Here I am not fully recovered, but wanting to have things nice for my man who had the audacity to do this. The next words out of his mouth were the words of a coward caught. "I don't want to do this anymore". I grabbed my stuff and I left. I couldn't believe I was playing this role of the girlfriend done wrong again. I started to rethink the decision I made to terminate this pregnancy. I thought I had someone that was going to be there for me. And now I don't have either. No baby, no man.

Over the next couple of days, severe depression set in. Here he is living his life, out in the world coning the next chick into thinking he was a stand-up man and I'm living in hell. That Friday, I was consumed with complete pity, shame and I just didn't want to do it anymore. That morning I packed a bag headed to work. Worked an 8 hour day, booked the best room in an NYC hotel. I took the elevator to the 27th Floor. Opened the door, took a shower opened my purse, and took out a bottle of pain medication and a bottle of Vodka. I stared at these two bottles for an hour before swallowing the whole bottle of pills and a glass of vodka. I blacked out. I awoke the next afternoon. I cried in the shower for 2 hours. I was still here. To this day, he doesn't know.

I didn't speak to him for a whole month before he called me wanting to talk. Working things out was never an option, but over time that's what seemed to be happening. Over the next year, there were good times and there were bad. It was beyond me why this man couldn't see what he had in a woman like me. His family would sing my praises to him. "I was a good woman, I was a beautiful woman, I was an intelligent woman" It didn't make sense. But I played the role. If they only knew what he had and still is putting me through they'd clutch their pearls and gold chains. It came to a point where every friend from the past was a suspect. And it came to the point where I was entertaining men outside of the relationship. I would make my rounds of cursing him and these bitches out on a monthly basis. It became a regular activity, like taking a shower. My weight fluctuated for months. I wasn't happy. He had no inkling of what I needed and what I wanted. He was so damaged confused and unhappy with himself that inflicting unhappiness on the one person that had his back and would quite possibly make him feel better. But I stayed, I stayed for several reasons: The very thought of starting over meeting and getting to know someone all over again depressed me. Like how many times do I have to do this before I get it right? I felt sorry for him on some weird level. We were raised in completely different households. Even though I grew up in a household that wasn't ideal as far as the affection displayed towards husband and wife, I grew to understand what it took. He never had that influence.

I knew how to treat a real man even though I was never in a relationship with one, I knew how to treat him. What would make him happy, he had no idea how to make a real woman feel wanted. I never asked him for a dime, I never ask for anything but his emotional presence and he either struggled to give it to me or just didn't want to. But hell, when you have women who weren't physically attractive falling for whatever an attractive yet severely damaged man was spitting to them, you tend to feel you don't have to work hard at anything. He felt important by breaking up with me whenever we didn't feel like putting effort into making things work. By this time, I lost 20lbs and was miserable. The depression I felt was a mixture of loneliness, guilt, fear. I was blank and vacant. I was declining hangouts with my friends to stay in bed and sleep off the pain. My second suicide attempt took place. This was the lowest point of my life. I wasn't strong enough to leave a situation and was desperate enough to end my life. Another failed relationship under my belt.

Rebuilding My Pretty

I started seeing a therapist 4 days later. This person was going to force me to confront every demon that is holding me back from being my beautiful, Intelligent, loving self. It was mandatory for my physical, emotional, mental wellbeing. I had to confront the disappointment of being mentally, emotionally, and physically abused, of being treated like an option and not a priority, being a beard to make these emotionally broken down men look good. It was me on some level, I didn't have the strength to see things for what they were, I didn't think much of myself to take care of me first then these men second. I gave all of me for a third of them. It had to stop. I had to realize "C" comes before "L" and "K". I also realized I had to rebuild my relationship with God. I needed him now more than ever. I put him on the back burner along with myself and it almost to one ticket to Hell. God deliberately denies access to things we want so bad so that he can provide us with the things we need. It s a matter of letting him do the job he never makes mistakes doing. I had to face the reality that I was beautiful just as much as I was flawed.... And that's ok! I had to keep moving and realize I was blessed beyond measure mainly because my heart is in the right place and most important I was given a second and third chance at life and to be happy . I have not given up on me as well as finding that true love I want and deserve but I am now better equipped with the wisdom and most important the self-respect and self-love I exchanged for that of a man. Your pretty is your own, it's not just how you wear it but how you project it. It is just a portion of the wonderful human being that you are deserving of all the happiness that you desire.

Pretty DEVASTATING

Chanee' Robinson

he grief lingers on in me still. All of the why's. All of the what if's.

What if he was part of my life?

What if he was there for my prom? Or my graduation? Or any birthdays?

What if the drugs did not have such a stronghold on him?

Would things have been different?

Why wasn't he there?

Why did he leave?

Why did he hit mommy?

What if he did not die before we were able to make amends?

And then there was the one-he stepped in and filled the void. For fifteen whole years, he was my Superman. The man who built my confidence. He taught me about self-worth and confidence. I felt spoiled beyond measure. He made me believe I could do anything. I could be anything.

A business owner. A father. A friend. I wanted for nothing. And then just like that, he was gone. Why?

Why did he allow us to grow so close if he didn't intend to be in my life forever?

What if he stayed in my life as an adult?

What if he met my little family?

What if you were my son's pop-pop?

Why didn't he see me cross the stage or walk down the aisle?

What if he would have stayed in my life after Mommy died?

These and a million other thoughts and questions run through my mind. . I grieve daily because of the questions whirling around in my head.

Let me start from my beginning.

Grief is an emotion I am all too familiar with.

The Merriam-Webster Dictionary defines grief in several different ways. The definition we have become accustomed to is the first one listed- “deep and poignant distress caused by or as if by bereavement”. Another definition reads, "an unfortunate outcome."

While I have written and talked about my feelings of grief about my mother's death in 2005, I have not expressed my feelings about the unfortunate outcome of not having a traditional father figure. Sure, I have a loving grandfather and uncles who have been there for me, but it’s different.

I often think about how my son does not have a living grandmother on my side; he also does not have a living grandfather on my side either. That hurts me. I do not have a parent for him to know, love, spend time with and be spoiled by. I rarely say things are unfair in my life, but not having parents to lean on as an adult does not seem right or fair, especially while everyone else around me has or have had those things. If your parent met your child, I have felt jealousy towards you. Seeing adults with their parents makes me feel jealous.

My Biological Father

My mother and biological father were married in 1980. I do not know much about their relationship before I came along, but I was born three years into their marriage. I am my mother's first child, and my father's second child, his first daughter.

My memories of him are few and far between, with 90% of them being negative. But 10% was good. I remember him bringing me fruit and candy home from work and being called baby girl. Although he did those things, I do not think I was ever a daddy's girl, but it is tough to say as both parents have now transitioned from this life. The other 90% are hard memories forever etched into my brain.

The abuse I witnessed still sticks with me until this day and has affected my view of the world and of people. And although that part was my mother's story to tell, the things I saw still stick with me and, as a result, was my experience to share.

I was three years old when I witnessed my father wrap his hands around my mother's neck. I believed he would kill her. All I could do was scream for Daddy to let go of Mommy. I remember nonchalantly recanting those details to my maternal grandmother. Imagine witnessing your father ball his fist up and try his best to punch your mother in her face. That time my uncle stopped him and I watched those two men, brothers, fight and tug, my mother right in the middle of them crying and screaming. I was doing the same because I was scared I couldn't help my mother. Imagine being held in a hotel room with your crying mother, infant brother.

During that incident, my mother woke my four-year-old self up. I was so confused. I remember asking where are we going? Why are we leaving Daddy? My mother pleaded with me to stop talking so we would not wake daddy up, who was sleep with a knife by the door so we could not getaway. We eventually escaped, but that was the day I lost trust in my father and police. The police who swore to protect us and keep us safe was rude to my mother as if she was lying.

The day Mommy finally had enough, she grabbed my brother and me, and we waited outside, maybe for a cab or bus, I cannot remember. As a little girl, I stood there, cold and relieved we were not going back into that apartment anymore.

These things happened in front of me when I was between three and four years old. No one retold these things to me; these are clear and distinct memories forever sketched into my brain.

As I got older, the memories were so much that I would often tell my mother I hate him. She would encourage me and tell me not to feel the way, but the pain was already ingrained in me, but I was too young to understand it let alone express it. When I was a teenager, I told my mother about my memories, and she could not believe I remembered so many things so clearly. I thought to myself, how could I ever forget?

I have not seen my biological father since my mother left him. I do know his family, my family- my grandmother, aunts, uncles, and cousins from my paternal side of the family. As a young child, my mother fostered that relationship. We saw my grandmother and aunts and uncles briefly for some holidays, and they would come to birthday parties. When my grandmother retired and bought a new house, my mother and I attended her celebrations and we attended family funerals. As a teenager and young adult, I began visiting and hanging out with my paternal family more frequently. I have male cousins in my age range who would visit me on campus at college or pick me up on the weekends and school breaks to hang out

I enjoyed getting to know that side of my family, but my biggest fear was running into my father. I had all this hate built up inside me, and I did not know what I would say or do if I ever had the chance. Sadly, that chance never came. In May of 2004, he passed away. At the time, I did not know how to feel. I did not initially cry. I guess I did not feel anything. It was not until I was sitting at my work-study job on campus that it all hit me, and I cried on another student's shoulder. I could not even explain what I was feeling. I did not know that man, the memories I have of him were violent, he never reached out to me, and there I was, twenty-one years old, a mess and crying because he died.

My aunt and uncles tried to paint a different picture of our relationship when he died. For the years I had visited them, went on shopping trips, and called them my father was never talked about. When he died my aunt tried to get me to write something to put in the obituary. When they were receiving visitors at the house during the week of his passing, they would proudly introduce me as his daughter. It was all so confusing and infuriating. They knew we did not have a relationship, but because their brother and son was gone I was supposed to go along with the fairytale they were trying to create.

I did not want to go to his funeral but decided to out of love and respect for my grandmother, who was burying another child. At the funeral, I could not build the nerve to even look inside his casket. I did not want to see him or even be there in the first place. I was told he looked just like my little brother lying in the casket. Another reason I did not want to look at him.

A few months after my biological father's passing my mother, my angel, my love, my rider-lost her four-and-a-half-year battle to ovarian cancer. It was that year that it hit me; I was an orphan. I did not just have some epiphany. When I filled out my FAFSA form and listed both my parents as deceased, the federal government labeled me an orphan. It was then I felt like I had been cheated. I had lost the most loving and supportive person in my life, and I did not have any parents left here on earth. I began to wish I had not spent years hating him. I learned so many lessons about myself and life from the feelings I started feeling back then.

My "Step" Father

For lack of a better term, I am going to tell you about my "stepfather." I put my step-father in quotations because my mother never remarried after leaving and officially divorcing my biological father.

She did get a boyfriend that I remember meeting when I was about six years old. He was a nice man, from what I could tell. Mommy seemed happy, and he seemed to care about us, my brother, and me. Real names are not necessary, so we'll refer to him as Mr. X.

Mr. X would take us to restaurants and buy us things and was overall nice to us. I do not remember the year it happened; my brother and I did not even discuss it. I remember one day, Mr. X coming over to the house and my and brother getting excited screaming Daddy! Daddy!

Mr. X and my mother looked surprised. I remember Mommy telling him she did not put us up to this and she did not. I guess me and my brother wanted a father and he had been around so long that we chose him. Mr. X must have been okay with his new role because from then on, I considered him Daddy. I finally had a father.

You could not tell me I was not a Daddy's girl. I would call on him for everything through the years, and I almost always got what I wanted. Every birthday was filled with several cards, balloons, and gifts. Christmas was out of this world; when we got too old for trick or treating, Mr. X would bring my brother, and me bags filled to the top with candy. He stepped right in and matched Mommy's energy as she had spoiled us as much as she could, too. While I was in college, I would call who I considered him and tell him I needed money to get my hair done or a ride to the grocery store, and he would make plans that week to get me what I needed. I am sure if Cash App were a thing twenty years ago, he would have received a weekly request from me.

But it was not all about his money or the things he did for us. That was an extension of his love. Mr. X is one of the people who built my confidence early on. Our family did not have people who dreamed very big. The few times I spoke about the dreams I had for my life, they were not met with the enthusiasm that I had expected as a young girl from members of my family. No one came out and said it, but you can feel people's energy, and I knew everyone in my family did not believe the things I believed about life. Do not get me wrong, my family is loving and proud, but it's hard for some people to see more than what is in front of them. Until Mr. X came into our lives, the only person I felt believed in every dream I had was my mother. He had shown that time and time again.

When I told Mr. X about my dreams, I got the same response as Mommy. He was excited for me. He made me believe I could do all I set out to do and more. In fourth grade, I began learning about government and elections. It was then I declared I would be the first woman president. Mr. X did not laugh or scoff but genuinely encouraged me and would refer to me as president. When I decided I would be an author and featured on Oprah’s book club, I had a family member tell me it was not possible, but not Mommy and Daddy. They believed in me and because of those two I kept believing and dreaming.

As I entered middle school, I remember Mr. X coming over or calling Mommy, and when he saw me or I answered the phone, he would always ask how I was doing. I would reply the same way every time, "I'm fine." And for years, his response would be, "I know you're fine, but how are you doing?" I would just laugh and think my daddy is so silly. What I learned later in life was this was his way of telling me I was beautiful. That is so important for young girls to hear from their father figures. He was boosting my self-esteem and self-confidence, and I did not realize it.

As I got older and interested in boys, he would talk to me about how men thought. At first, it was the scare tactic that most men use. He told me not to trust any of the boys; they were all dirty. I would smile and nod nervously and say okay. But then he became real when it was time for me to go to college. He talked to me about protecting myself and trusting men. Those conversations were so uncomfortable for me, but as I reflect so necessary, and shaped who I would become as a young woman.

My mother was diagnosed with ovarian cancer when I was a junior in high school. Looking back, Mr. X was not the supportive man that stood by his woman's side. If I am honest, the entire relationship was not ideal, but I did not know that as a young girl. The sicker she got, the less he was around for her, but I could not see because I felt like my dad was still there for me. I was going into college and eventually moved onto campus for three years. I was not home to witness the toll Mommy's illness took on their relationship. I did not know he was not there for her or supportive. As I still saw him at the time, my dad was always there for me when I called for a ride, money, and advice. He even showed up for my birthdays, gave me whatever I asked for, and answered every time I called. My mother, just like she did with my biological dad, never spoke an ill word about Mr. X to me. He was still my dad up until her death.

I had gotten wind of how their relationship deteriorated from family. I did not get involved or caught up in it. I did not know what to think or believe. I was too busy convincing myself Mommy would get better, and everything would go back to the way they were before, but they never did.

After Mommy passed, I stayed in contact with Mr. X. At the time, he was still dad. A few months later, I moved out of the house I grew up with my mother, brother, and grandparents. My grandparents and brother still lived there, but I could not take it anymore, so my aunt helped me get my first apartment. I felt so grown up and was so proud. I called dad to tell him about it as I did with all of my big news. By this time, his business had failed, and he had started working for someone else. I was twenty-two years and a little more mature and had stopped asking for every little thing from him. After hearing all about my new apartment, he asked if I had furniture yet. I told him I did. I had fully furnished the place when I moved in. He asked how much my living room set cost; I told him eight hundred dollars. He told me he would pay for it. He would get paid that Friday, give me five hundred dollars, then the rest when he got paid in two more weeks. I want to reiterate he asked me and volunteered this money; I did not ask, hint, or tell him I needed anything. I excitedly accepted the offer and thanked him. He told me he would call me that Friday to come to see my new place and give me the money.

That was June 2005. That was the last time I spoke to Mr. X.

It took me a few years to deal with what happened with Mr. X. I went through a phase of hating him like I did my biological father. Through reflection and therapy, I was able to find meaning and gain lessons from losing my second father.

The Lessons Led To Growth

I was a child and young adult when I went through these lessons, but a mature woman on the path to bettering herself when I finally understood them.

My trust issues and the wall I built around me emotionally come from the loss of my parents. In the past, I wondered why me? Why did I have to witness abuse? Why didn't I get to grow up with a father in the house? As cliché' as it sounds, God doesn't put more on you than you can bear. I can now understand God has equipped me with tools like access to therapy and the opportunity to share my experience in this book to help others because He knew I could handle it, even when I thought I could not.

What I have learned is everyone deals with demons, some worse than others. I may never know why my biological dad turned to drugs. I will not know what he went through in his life and what he was trying to escape being a young black man growing up in Baltimore in the eighties. I do not make excuses for him or blame myself for our lack of relationship while he was here, but I do wish I did not spend so many years hating and avoiding him.

The impact of having and losing father figures, literally and figuratively, has directly impacted how I approached relationships as an adult. During my dating years I would not take men with children seriously. I was adamant about it. At the time I did not realize it, but I know that it was for two reasons. I did not see fathers as dependable and someone who would be there for you and love you unconditionally. I knew I could not date or respect someone who was not there for their child in the way I thought they should be. To avoid all of the drama I avoided all men with children. I have heavily judged men who are not there for their children full-time.

I have learned the importance of being there for your child in any way you can. No matter how wonderful one parent is, children thrive even more when they can have both in their life. It does not matter if the romantic relationship between the parents has deteriorated. Children, boys, and girls need their dads. Make every effort to be there. Don't block a parent who wants to be there and support your significant other's relationship with their children. It's so important.

I have learned the importance of communication. I would tell the few people that I trust how my stepfather had not called me since June 2005, but I never called him either. I was used to being catered to and being the child. I expected him to check up on me and still be there for me, especially since I had just lost my mother. I blamed him because I lost all three parents within a year of each other, except he was still here; he is still here last I heard.

Both fathers taught me, directly and indirectly, what not to put up within a relationship. From watching them mistreat my mother and not give her everything I believe she deserved I knew exactly what I did not want in a man. So much so that I was sometimes unnecessarily harsh. That harshness helped weed out a lot of foolishness. My standards and expectations were so high that only people often weeded themselves out.

Lastly, I have learned how important it is to forgive others and let go of the hurt and the pain. I have done that, worked on myself, and have been a much better person for it. It is not up to children to foster relationships with their parents, but I will say leave a little room in your heart to forgive. Even if you do not want them in your life, leave a place to forgive for your growth.

Pretty HURTS
Skyler Freeman

Growing up as the oldest of seven children, how pretty I looked was not something I truly put much effort or thought into. I was too busy making sure my siblings Simone and Nicie were well taken care of. You see, my mom was already an alcoholic by the time I was five; due to losing her baby sister in a drug transaction gone wrong, so I was always the caregiver of the family and honestly it suits my personality well. Nurturing, providing, and caring for others is a gift I've learned to utilize to my advantage. When the world seems so cold to my family and friends, I enjoy being warm, cause that's how my stepmom and grandmother always made me feel growing up, warm, and cared for. So naturally, I adopted their characteristics as my own and grew up exuding that to others. The only thing about that is, people who are insecure with themselves can not accept the love and the gifts that come with you. I had to learn that in the most daunting way one can imagine.

I remember distinctly working at the Dallas County Sheriff's department, in the bonds and warrants office. I was twenty-six years old and in love with this guy who was tall, dark, and handsome in my eyes. However, I was unaware that he came with baggage of an insecure ex-girlfriend, whom by the way I could not tell you what she looks like to this day. This relationship felt like the one, like they all do in the beginning, and this guy and I did everything together.

I knew at 26 years old he was very interested in me and cared for me. He enjoyed taking me to Victoria's Secret and spending time with me and my boys; I was feeling his vibes the same. I enjoyed his company and what felt like companionship as well. You couldn't tell me that this relationship wasn't going to be successful. But his ex had other plans for our relationship. About six months into our relationship, he called me asking me about a guy at the job that his ex said I talk to. Yes, his ex was behind this. I honestly was dumbfounded. What grown man believes what his ex has to say about his new girlfriend? Well, to my surprise that was only the beginning of a romantic relationship going downhill. After that, this woman had "text message" receipts of me going back and forth with another man at our place of work, and she even went as far as having a guy that she knows stalk me. It was the scariest thing I have ever been through, to have a complete stranger hate you for no reason.

I had a breakdown in my bathroom floor cause I had never experienced a trauma like that. Being a victim of lies, deceit, and betrayal all because an ex was insecure. It was hard and my relationship with God wasn't as solid as it should have been, which caused me to go into a deep depression. Being falsely accused is wrong within itself, but when someone you don't know can blatantly lie to you, that's another form of how low an individual with insecurities will go. I was mentally and emotionally scared, not knowing that in three more years I would face an even worse ex to overcome. In late 2016, I met a man in Walmart who followed me throughout the store to get my number. I thought it was cute, and like the other, he was tall and handsome and said he was single, so I gave him my number.

We had the same chemistry late nights, early mornings, on the phone, you name it. The thing with this relationship is that we moved way too fast and because again my relationship with God was nowhere how it needed to be. I was vulnerable to walk in the flesh and not in the spirit. We became intimate within a month. I didn't give him time to show me he truly cared for me, which was a fault of my own. My love and kindness were both extended almost immediately to a stranger. A stranger that, three months later, I would get pregnant by. I didn't know this man, the lack of love I had for myself made me believe that love came from someone else. Other than dating and spending nights alone, I didn't know the baggage that he would bring into my life. Shortly after I announced to him I was pregnant, he seemed happy when we were together, so I proceeded to convince myself that having a baby with someone that I barely knew was best for me and the two kids I already had. It was then I was haunted again with the same atrocities of an ex that had control, only this time I was in too deep. This man only spoke briefly about his ex but because I was not one to ask many questions, I honestly didn't listen. It was when I was due that I received a Facebook phone call from who I believed was his ex living in Kansas City, Missouri. She advised me how he told her he was going to put me out once I had the baby. Not only that, but she also mentioned that she was coming to Texas to move in with him. I couldn't take anything this woman was saying seriously because I was the one that was pregnant. I was the one that he was preparing to have a baby with. Soon after, he received a phone call and went outside to talk privately.

I watched him from the window and witnessed how scared, shocked, and confused he looked. I was speechless. He came in the house and reassured me that everything that she was saying was lies, his daughter that they had together was sick, and that he was leaving for Kansas City. I couldn't believe my ears. I knew that this man was lying to me but I was already nine months pregnant, I lost my car and honestly was at the lowest point I had ever been with him.

Due to my emotional exhaustion, I did not fight him leaving. I only asked him to drop me off at my mom's and hoped I wouldn't go into labor while he was away. On October 10, 2017, I went into labor. He had just got back from Kansas City, too. Giving birth to my first girl was to be the most beautiful moment of my life, but I was faced with giving birth to my daughter while her dad stayed on the phone with another woman almost the entire time. I was in complete shock because this man was crying and it wasn't for the joy that he had just brought another life into this world, but that his ex and the daughter that they had were facing eviction and needed a place to live. He was crying as if his life was about to end. I asked him where I was supposed to go with this newborn baby because my mom was living with her husband so there was no room for me there, and my sisters both were in estranged relationships. I honestly had nowhere to go. He promised me that he would figure it out and I believed that he would. So, me and my newborn daughter went to his place. For some strange reason, the holy spirit was telling me to leave, but I wouldn't listen. This man was acting strange when me and the baby got there. He would sleep on the floor and when the baby would cry he acted as if she wasn't there.

After being there for only one week with the baby, I received another phone call from his ex. This time, she was asking me why was I still there when they had just had sex on October 10th. She said that he promised her that me and the baby would be out. I was heartbroken and crushed and couldn't believe my ears. He denied it all but I had had enough. I called my little sister to come and pick me up and left that night. Shortly after, I received another phone call. This time it was the ex's sister asking can we meet to fight, and how they had just thrown out me and the baby's stuff. I looked at the phone and hung up. I called the Lewisville, TX police department to file a complaint and, to my surprise, the dispatcher had advised me that there was already an arrest made at the address that I provided.

A domestic violence call was made and my daughter's dad and his ex were arrested. Turns out she was actually in town with her U-Haul truck and family to move into the same apartment that me and this man were sharing. The windows were busted out and there was an altercation between the two. It was unfathomable to believe that the man that I carried a baby for had no intention of providing or protecting me or his innocent child.

Shortly after his release, he asked that I give him some time to let things calm down before me and the baby came back. When I went to get clothes a few days later while he was at work, his ex was there with her sisters and cousins. I almost lost my mind. Even after being jailed due to his ex, he ultimately moved her in. Me and my 4-week old baby had nowhere to go, so we went to Arlington Life Shelter to live. I had no hope, no money, and honestly had no will to live. My postpartum depression sank in heavily and I was traumatized. So many nights in that cold shelter I wanted to take me and my baby girl's life. I felt I failed as a mother and didn't want her to endure a life of hell and being a fatherless little girl. But something inside of me wouldn't let me do it. This baby was special, always smiling and happy I could not hurt her. I could only give her my unconditional love. It was a hard pill to swallow. My boys share the same father, so they had a present father, but this innocent, beautiful 4 week old baby was in my arms and already rejected by her own father. I didn't know where to pick up the pieces of my life. I knew that at that moment only one who I could run to was God. The shelter was a Christian environment and Wednesdays was bible study. I would go with my newborn baby and hear God's words. Scared and alone, me and my baby only left our dorm to use the bathroom, and leave during the time everyone had to be out. The staff would always ask if they could play with my baby. They were all amazed by her, she actually made people happy!

There was one sweet worker who would not leave until after she saw my daughter. My hope for humans began to come alive again. I began to go to church and became a member of the Potter's House in Fort Worth, TX. It was in those walls that I found out who I was and whose I was. My life changed going to that church. It fed my soul and filled my spirit. My insecurities were rooted way back from childhood. Having a mother that was too drunk to be present and a father I never knew, I actually never had high self-esteem. No one told me that I was beautiful as a young girl, so I grew up to be a woman walking around existing. Letting my love go to whoever pretended to care. But in putting my focus into learning God's words and laws, I was found and healed. The process of forgiving and letting God's love is not easy. In fact, it was extremely hard. Many nights, I screamed out to God to take the pain away, but he didn't. I endured all of it. I felt every emotion of living in the flesh; unbearable pain, emotional pain, physical pain, financial loss. It all had to be washed away and run its course, for him to be present in my life and in me. I had monthly meetings with counselors at the church to stay focused on God and not fall into any fleshly ways like seeking revenge. I had learned that revenge is for God to take care of not me.

My heavenly Father was calling out to me and I couldn't ignore it. I had to change my focus and direction in life in order to heal. God is holy and his holiness can not exist with fleshy spirits. I was weak for love, and I believed any man that said that he loved me so I was available to him. It was after the unimaginable pain I was able to see God's goodness and walk beside him.

The love that he gave me was a love I had never experienced with any other human being. It's a secure love that won't run out because of an ex or leave me stranded and abandoned. I experience unthinkable loss by men who had insecure exes and ultimately weak and insecure themselves. But God's love is secure! His love promises to provide and protect me from all harm and shelter me when I have nowhere to go. It was during my time learning and loving God, I noticed the healing in my life. The peace that was brought in with each new day was new to me.

I used to constantly worry about things but loving God and accepting Jesus as my savior brought on a new kind of serenity that I had never experienced. It was good and I wanted more. I was able to slowly get back on my feet. I had found a one-bedroom apartment with my baby when she was six months old. I purchased a car and I was able to see where I had gone wrong in life.

God was not my priority before the tragedies and had he been the outcomes would have been different. I am aware of that now. Bible study is my new normal; singing songs of praise and worship started to be the only songs I need to hear, watching faith-filled shows is the only thing I need to watch.

Praying daily with my children also is a priority. My creativity is back inside me. I'm dreaming big and journaling daily. Creativity flows through me, and it is my outlet to transform the pain into something beautiful, just like God had done with me. My walk with God is a transformation from insecure to secure, from being lost to being found from being broken to healed. Even though I'm not where he has told me I'm going, I'm dedicated to enjoy this journey with.

Pretty LOST
Tiffany Fosmire-Mathias

It was May 1994. I sat on the floor of my grandmother's bathroom. In my trembling right hand, I held a pregnancy test. As I waited for the plus sign to appear and confirm what I already knew, my mind wandered to the other room. It was the bedroom that I shared with my grandmother. There was an invisible line that divided the room in half. On one side my grandmother's bed and her belongings, me on the other. At 18 years old it wasn't the optimum situation to be living in, but it was far better than some of the places I had previously slept. I was content and I felt safe.

Closing my eyes, I could see my bed freshly made, pillows fluffed, throw blanket folded, and placed neatly at the foot of the bed. All of my toiletries were perfectly lined up on the dresser, the labels facing outward and in size order. The mirror was recently cleaned and streak-free. In the top right drawer, sitting next to my bras and panties sat my acceptance letter to Hofstra University as an Early Childhood Education major. Order. I needed; no I craved order. There were so many things in my life that I had little to no control of or say so over. I had to grab hold of something in the tornado that was my existence and have it make sense. I had to make sure that regardless of the inner turmoil, confusion, and dysfunction that had been my life, I had to present to the outside world I had my shit together. I opened my eyes, chest-pounding, tears burning to fall, it was confirmed.....PREGNANT!

My mind raced to put all the pieces in place. College! A baby! What am I going to do? What would my family think? What are my friends going to say? What is HE going to say? What will HIS family say? Think? I couldn't breathe. So there I sat for only God knows how long. I cried. I laughed. I laid on the floor flailing my arms and legs like a toddler having a temper tantrum. I wished to go back to that day that this happened (I knew EXACTLY when it happened) and do something different. "I knew your fast ass should have stayed home!!!", I chastised myself. I had a conversation with God. I tried negotiating. I told him if I did the test again because OBVIOUSLY, THIS ONE WAS WRONG, I'd never have unprotected sex again. I think he knew I was lying. I prayed for him to "take it back". I wasn't ready for this precious gift he had given me. Then I cursed myself for even thinking such thoughts. I weighed my options, abortion, adoption, accidental miscarriage (did I have it in me to "trip and accidentally fall down a flight of stairs"). I think I may have actually cried myself to sleep because sometime later I heard my grandmother call my name.

I got up off the floor, wrapped my secret in toilet paper, and put it gently in my pocket. I washed my face and went to watch game shows with my grandmother. This was part of our nightly routine. We'd watch Wheel of Fortune and Jeopardy and shout out the answers to the puzzles. That night I couldn't concentrate. I didn't attempt to answer one puzzle or answer one question. I zoned out a couple of times and pictured myself on the television as a contestant.

Alex, "Get's pregnant and ruins her life"

Me, "Who is, Tiffany Fosmire"

When I woke up the next morning I hoped the events of the previous day were just a dream. I reached for jeans and pulled out the wad of toilet paper and unwrapped its contents. Nope, it wasn't a dream. I laid in the bed knowing in my heart my decision had already been made. I just needed to put my big girl panties on and see it through. It probably took me two weeks to muster up the courage to have the conversations with the people I needed to. Some of the conversations were easier than others. The most difficult of them was with my grandfather. My grandfather was my first hero and the first man in my life to not turn his back on me or let me down. He was an old school, old fashioned man. He was stern and though he was probably only five feet and six inches tall, his presence dominated every room he entered. I sat down with him one Saturday afternoon. He was watching an old John Wayne movie. I remember creeping into the dark living room and sitting down in a chair in the corner. I told him I needed to talk to him and it was important. He motioned for me to turn the television off and come sit next to him. I walked tentatively towards the tv and turned it off. When I sat down next to him, I just knew he could hear my heart pounding in my chest. Between a downpour of tears and heavy breathing, I told him. He asked if I planned to marry the father. He questioned my future and my intentions for going to college. I didn't have answers for him because I couldn't answer the questions for myself. All I could promise him, promise myself was that ONE DAY I would go to school and when I did finally graduate with my degree, my child would be in the audience cheering me on.

The next few years were tough. I decided not to attend Hofstra. Instead, I focused on my pregnancy and having a healthy baby. I moved back home with my parents and 5 younger siblings at my mother's insistence. I got a job working at Dr. Jay's, a popular urban clothing and sneaker store in the Tri-State area. I started as a sales associate in the shoe department. It was probably one of the worst jobs. It wasn't a commission job but I did use to my advantage my growing belly. While assisting the customers I would place the box on my growing belly. My poor attempt at getting customers to be empathetic towards my condition and not waste my time. My manager at the store was Victor, and he was probably the greatest manager I ever had. He was very caring about my condition but he also was very nurturing. I can recall a conversation he had with me one day before I left for my maternity leave. I was due January 20th and my last day scheduled was January 6th. In retail, right after the Christmas holiday, merchandise goes on clearance, and preparation for a physical inventory starts. I was helping Victor with the inventory paperwork and he asked me, " So after you have this baby, are you coming back to work? What do you want to do with your life? What type of life are you preparing for you and the baby?" I almost cried. It was January and I had no better answers that day than I did back in May. He told me to use my time home to not only bond with my newborn but also set some goals. When I returned to work, WE had work to do. Can I tell you I was flabbergasted. First of all, this man wasn't any type of relation to me. He was my boss. I was his employee. According to him, he'd been doing his job for YEARS. So he'd seen plenty of young ladies come and go. However, for some unknown reason, he saw something different in me. Something obviously I wasn't seeing in myself, yet. There wasn't any guarantee or assurance that I would be returning to that job. It was a minimum wage retail job, but Victor had an expectation. He'd given me a challenge and let me tell you, I do love a good challenge.

I gave birth to a beautiful baby girl a couple of weeks later. She was perfect. 10 fingers. 10 toes. And equipped with a set of lungs like no other. Being the eldest of my siblings and cousins, I just knew motherhood was going to be a piece of cake. Wrong again. My daughter was an active child. Initially I had difficulties getting her to nurse. I felt like a failure when she didn't latch. It was very important to me that I nursed her. I wanted that bond. My mother and aunts were very supportive. For days, I squeezed the colostrum onto my nipples, hoping she would catch. I would cry everytime she didn't and gave in to the nurses and presented my infant with a bottle. My aunt Jennie came to visit my last day in the hospital. She reassured me that I could do it, that the baby picked up on my energy and that I needed to stay the course and not get upset or the baby would too. So on my last feeding before we were discharged I presented my extremely engorged breast to my hungry baby. When she caught that nipple I hollered. I immediately went to snatch her off. THAT WAS A HUGE MISTAKE. It only caused my hungry- hungry hippo to suck harder. With patience and resilience I learned my first lesson in parenting.

I don't know what I would have done without the support of my family. My mother was incredible. She was there for me every step of the way as I cared for my newborn. All the things I thought I knew about raising kids and how to care for an infant went right out the window. Sure I knew the basics and I was very nurturing, however, when that baby is your own and there is no one else there to tag in when you're tired or just need a moment to yourself it's easy to feel defeated and like a failure. One thing my mother was firm on was that this is MY baby and she belonged to me and I was responsible for her. She was not going to allow me to fail.

Three months came and went so quickly and then it was time for me to return to work. I was anxious and excited to be back to work but nervous about leaving my baby. My mother was going to watch her while I went to work, I at least knew she was in safe hands and not with a stranger. Don't think I got over though. I was paying for this service, $50/week. Returning to work I was ready to take on the challenge previously set before me by my manager. I was also experiencing a serious cabin fever. I missed engaging with my peers and co-workers. I even missed dealing with the public. There is something to be said about working in customer service. It will try your patience and have you question your religion. You meet people from all over the world, people who speak different languages and make connections with people with some of the most interesting stories.

Upon my return to work, I realized that I wanted more. Victor reminded me of our last conversation. We got to work cross-training me on every job in the store. When the truck arrived with daily inventory, there I was counting in the boxes and cross-checking them off the shipping manifest. Once the boxes were in, I was taught how to process them. This meant, stripping the manufacturer's packaging, hanging, folding, price tagging, attaching sensors to prevent theft but not damage the garment at the same time. From there it was floor rotation and visual merchandising. Once those skills were mastered, I was trained for the registers, then became the trainer, and finally, I worked with the opening and closing managers to balance the registers and prepare the deposits for armored car service. I also had a crash course in management and conflict resolution when 2 associates got into a physical altercation in the store.

One of my favorite tasks in the store was merchandising. From pulling together the outfits and merchandise to go in the windows, to mannequins in the store or the way a 4-way was set was fascinating to me. Merchandising...the silent salesman. Without saying a word, I had the ability to sell you a look based on how it was presented to you. Placing the right items in the window drew customers into the store. Dressing the mannequins felt like playing with life-size Barbie dolls. During one of these merchandising sessions with a vendor, I learned that you could actually go to school, get a degree, and get a high paying job to do this. Wait! What? I can get paid for playing with dolls and expressing my creativity. Where do I sign up?

I applied to college within a month of that conversation. I didn't tell anyone because I didn't want to be rejected and have others share in my setback and disappointment. Every day I got up and went to work. At this point in time, Victor was no longer with the company and his replacements were not like him. They were strict. They were rude and did not know how to talk to people. Everything that was said to the employees sounded like a demand. Granted yes, they were management, but there is a way to give a subordinate a direction without making them feel less than or give what I would later learn in my career is called feedback and redirection. Many of the coworkers I had gotten close to started quitting or transferred to other stores. That wasn't my plan. I waited and waited for a letter to come that would send me in my next direction. That letter came at the end of June 1997. When I opened the letter from CUNY (City University of New York) my heart pounded in my ears. Quickly glancing over the letter I searched for keywords like CONGRATULATIONS, WELCOME,

AND OUR PLEASURE. There they were. I had been accepted to CUNY-City Tech as an incoming undergrad majoring in Fashion Marketing!!!! I rushed up the stairs tripping over the last two and falling onto the floor.

My mother looked at me from the kitchen table like I was crazy. She asked what was wrong with me. I just kept repeating, "I got in! I GOT IN!!!"

"In what?"

"College, mom. I'm going to college"

The smile that spread across her face was priceless. She hugged me hard, kissed my face, and said she was proud of me. I resigned from the store two weeks later. Now I'm not quite sure why I thought that was the best move. I still had a toddler to care for and school to pay for. I took this acceptance letter as my freedom papers. I didn't have to be stuck in a dead-end retail job. Classes were starting at the end of August and I had a few weeks to figure things out. How I was going to pay for it, plan my schedule, and get my daughter settled into a new routine.

Since I had been out of school for four years, I had to take something called a CUNY proficiency exam. It was a multi-part test in mathematics, ELA, and writing. Based on my scores from this test, I would be able to schedule my classes. Stepping onto the campus I felt empowered and walked with a different strut in my steps. My steps were more purposeful. I didn't just have a physical destination to get to, but a life one. I scored high on the ELA and writing but missed passing math. I would need to take a remedial math class to bring me to the college level required before I could take my first college-level math class. A minor misstep in my path but I was ready.

I was able to get financial aid to help pay for school and got approved for a work-study program. This allowed me to earn money between classes working in one of the offices on campus. I worked in the advisory office. As part of the staff in the advisory office, it was my responsibility to schedule appointments for students with their academic advisors. The number of students that passed through the office because they were in jeopardy of being placed on academic probation was frightening. Most of the students attending this college received some sort of financial aid to attend and it was quite saddening to see many of them wasting the money and the opportunity because they didn't have their priorities together. I had to constantly remind myself that they weren't like me. They weren't bringing a toddler to school with them and signing them into daycare. They weren't up to the wee hours of the night, studying at the kitchen table when the house was finally quiet. They weren't working a second job on the weekends to supplement the income from work-study because they needed to buy pull-ups, wipes and the baby had outgrown yet another pair of sneakers. This was my story. These were my circumstances. I had to focus on my journey and not worry about anyone else's.

By the completion of my 4th semester, I was excelling. I was on the Dean's List. I had also added to my laundry list of responsibilities, The International Business Organization aka IBO. It was a student activities program geared towards business majors to help them connect with and foster relationships in the business world. It was also one of the most popular organizations on the campus and was known for producing a dope AF end of year variety show which showcased the talents of the students and local entertainers. I also completed that semester with an acceptance to a summer internship program at MACY'S. I was on cloud nine. The feeling of pride, the sense of accomplishment I had in myself almost made me forget that a mere 4 years or so ago, many people in my family and even a few close friends, had me written off as just another statistic.

That summer internship was nothing at all I dreamed it would be. There were times I felt like a glorified cashier and stock girl. I was taken back to my days as a salesperson and cashier at Dr. Jay's. I wasn't well-liked by the manager I was training under either. I never knew why. This intelligent woman of color was placed in a position where she was to be a trainer/mentor and failed horribly at it. If I did everything by the book, I was told that I would not succeed without using my brain. If I thought outside the box, I was reprimanded for not following directions. When I sought help, I was told she didn't have time and to figure it out. Every week I was asked by the program director how things were going and if I needed any help. Every week I smiled and reassured them things were great. It wasn't until I was placed in the same role years later that I realized why I did it. Subconsciously, I knew the harm it would have done to her career and mine. In a white male dominating world, the last thing I needed to present to the company was two minority women tearing each other down. I would have not done myself or this woman any justice. Sometimes in life, we meet and work with people with who we just don't get along with. For 8 weeks I busted my behind to complete my training manual and submit my assignments on time and with little to no help from the woman who was supposed to guide me. At the completion of my internship, I was offered a position. This was wonderful, except I had two more semesters to complete before I received my degree and between my course load and parenthood, I wasn't ready to put all that on myself. I respectfully declined the offer and returned to school.

When the fall semester came, I ran for president of the IBO. I came in second and became Vice President. With that title came the responsibility of being the chairwoman for the end of year show. Finishing my last two semesters became a challenge. My classes got harder. Who would have thought? Balancing my time between fundraising, scheduling meetings, holding auditions, working, and being a parent, my grades slipped, DRASTICALLY. I was faced with some tough decisions. In order to maintain my financial aid, I had taken on extra courses. It was quite unsettling when I received my first D grade on an assignment. I looked at the foreign grade next to my name and made a decision. I dropped the class. After that things went smoothly again. I gracefully finished both the fall and spring semesters.

It was time to finish things off.

Many choices and decisions had to be made. I placed deadlines upon myself that only intensified my need to end this part of my journey on a high note. I was faced with the choice of finishing my degree and moving on to my career. Or, I could then transfer to another school and pursue my bachelor's. I also wanted to move into my own apartment with my daughter and be independent. Lastly, I needed the IBO show to be the best show ever as I was adding all the work details and skills to my resume. The pressures I placed upon myself were immeasurable. Some nights, I barely got 3 hours of sleep.

I constantly felt tired. Not sleepy, but tired. I was falling asleep in my classes. I had no days off. I was going to school Monday through Thursday. Holding rehearsals three days a week. Working in the advisory office for four days and then working in a boutique on the weekends. I was so close to accomplishing so many goals that I was burning the candle at both ends and was about to crash. When it came time to take my finals I was cramming, a study tactic I knew didn't work well for me. By the grace of the Most High, I passed. I got 1 C plus, 2 Bs, and an A-minus. The night of the show came and with hiccup and mishap one after another, the show went on. To my amazement, the audience loved it. Score another win for me. Finally, graduation day arrived.

On a scorching hot day in June, my mother, father, grandmother, and daughter sat in the audience at Madison Square Garden. I waited in line in the hallway with the thousands of other graduate candidates for my major to be called in. When the announcement was made for the graduates with an Associates in Applied Science in Fashion Marketing to march in I silently wept. My heart swelled as I entered the auditorium. Once I reached my seat, I released a sigh of relief. I had done it. I wasn't a statistic any longer. I was an educated woman with a career path before me and a purpose.

I decided to take a full-time position working at the boutique. I was working with a woman, Mimi, who was teaching me hands-on buying and planning. I learned the ins and outs of small business management. Her business was her baby and she treated her employees like family. I received from this woman the mentorship and guidance I didn't receive during that previous summer's internship. I stayed with Mimi for two years. When the time came for me to make my next move, I received praise and reassurance that if I ever needed her, she would be there for me.

A few years later, I ended up back at Macy's. This time I was the manager. I was the mentor. When I was told I was going to be receiving a summer internship, I grumbled. I didn't have time to spoon-feed some eager college kid. Then I heard Victor and Mimi's voices in my head, "It's now your turn to show them what WE taught you." I was about to treat this intern the same way I had been treated. I learned it was actually a privilege to be selected as a training manager. Not only did my direct manager nominate me, but I was approved by the store manager and the regional management team. This meant my career was being watched. I was being groomed for new opportunities. That's not something that happens for everyone.

On my road to happiness, I have hit some roadblocks and had to recalibrate my route many times. Matter of fact, as I write this anthology, I am finding myself being redirected from what I thought was my next stop to happiness. I am truly blessed for not only my wins in my but also my losses. My takeaway from these hardships are as follows:

1. You define your own happiness and you don't have to explain it to anyone but yourself.
2. We are our own harshest critics. Nobody can tear you down faster than you can. So speak words of positivity into yourself every day. Especially in those darkest of times.
3. Happiness is not a destination. It is a journey. What brings one happiness today, may not do so tomorrow. Be open to change.

4. Be kind. Regardless of where you are in your life, someone is looking up to you for guidance. Be a beacon and shine on.
5. Lastly, love yourself, your whole self. Nobody will ever be able to fill the void you leave in yourself.

Pretty SINGLE
Jazzy Kash

Born in the Washington D.C area in the nineties to a single mother and an absent father, Jazzy was forced to become very independent at an early age. Growing up wasn't always easy but that never stopped Jazzy from accomplishing her goals and becoming a woman who inspires many young women. Her resilience and determination allowed her to overcome many of life's obstacles all while pursuing her dreams and being a good friend and family member. As Jazzy embarks on her thirties, she shares some of the life lessons that have become etched into her mind like her favorite song to forever remind her of her journey to self-discovery and love. Have you ever heard the common saying "don't go looking for love"? It's not a coincidence that over many years, this saying has become popular. You may have heard it because oftentimes we naturally can overlook what we are looking for, even when it's right in front of us. When we go actively looking for love, and we haven't taken the time to find ourselves first, our perspective of things can become cloudy. When we finally do experience love we aren't able to see it because we are observing from the wrong state of mind or with the wrong intentions. If you aren't able to see love, most times you aren't able to love properly, because you won't be able to recognize it at all. You may ask, how can you experience self-love and romantic love at the same time? The answer is to set your intentions on self-love and romantic love will follow. Setting your intentions starts with understanding what you need rather than what you want out of a relationship or partnership. When you go looking for love in others that you have not first built within you are essentially only wasting your time. So many people believe that they want to be in a relationship, and they yearn for love so badly that they often do not realize that companionship has to come from the right person and at the right time in your life.

Oftentimes we meet someone and they make us feel loved, and then only by getting closer to them, we realize that who we thought they were is not what we in all actuality needed. We sometimes think we are ready for a relationship and that later learn that the person may have baggage that you weren't aware of. You come to a place where you have to decide if this is something that you need in your life at that time. If you decide to pursue a relationship with this person and they cannot offer you something that you need, that can prevent them from being available to you in certain ways that you require. When two people decide to commit to each other, there must be a constant give and take that must take place in order for the love locomotion to progress into the various stages of a relationship. We will go further into the relationship stages later. By committing to something that you don't need at the wrong time in your life, you are only going to hurt yourself in the long run. Through trial and error, I learned to determine my needs and desires by setting standards and by reinforcing those with boundaries of stages in the along-term relationship. Learning what I needed at every stage of my relationship, helped me to decipher between who was qualified to be a love interest and who was better off as friends, and who I had to cut out of my life completely.

A Lot of us like to think that we are always in the right place at the right time and that by fate we will meet the right person. However, life is not always that simple, and if we aren't careful we can get so wrapped up in the idea that we can miraculously fall in love by fate, so much that we can overlook what's right in front of us. We can stay in the wrong place for so long, and by not noticing that it is actually wrong for us and leaving, we stick around hoping things will change. This doesn't mean that you cannot still manage to get back on track and meet the love of your life at the perfect time. Dating in my twenties was a challenge mainly because I believed that I was always in the right place and making the right decisions. I was stubborn and stuck in my ways, every choice I made was justified and valid and any mistake was chalked up to simply choosing the wrong person. Not everyone you date is the wrong person for you, but everyone you date also isn't the forever person for you. When I began to date in stages I was able to hold back feelings in exchange for thinking logically and not with my heart. Everyone you encounter has a lesson to teach you and something to offer you. If you are able to decipher through the bullshit that comes with meeting new people and view them as people along your journey, there are all different types of people, from all walks of life that can teach you something about themselves, yourself, and life in general. By getting to know people beyond sex and attraction, you are able to save yourself time and effort because everything has to progress in its own time.

Love should not be rushed or imitated and should only come from a genuine place of adoration and care. The first lesson I learned the hard way was to take my time to get to know a person's character, behaviors, family, and friends before initiating the next stage of the relationship beyond attraction: Friendship. Previously I would rush into relationships, and by switching to my new slow and steady philosophy I had to unlearn many habits. One of the biggest lessons along the way was the importance of timing. There always comes a time when you have to do something different and change is necessary for growth. When we are patient with the speed at which we and the things around us are growing, we will see that everyone is moving at their own pace and tempo. If we stop growing by changing, you will soon see how life will not wait for you. You may lose people and opportunities that were once at arms reach are further away.

As an adult, you have to always be prepared for when

challenges arise, as they always do. We have people who are in your corner but if you stop growing, people often grow apart and it can seem as if it has happened for no reason. The fact is that no matter what choices we make in life, it will always continue and no one is required to stay in one place for anyone.

Life is about finding your vibe and riding your own wave to the beat of your own band. Will you be a one-man-band or have an entire orchestra that harmonizes beautifully? Every piece of your pie has to fit perfectly and when things in your life are not balanced and working in harmony, your life will not taste sweet. Making changes along the way is inevitable and can be difficult to navigate at times. One way to stay on track is to remember that time is always of the essence and communication is key. Are you filling your time with people and things that bring you joy and happiness? Are you occupying your time with the things that you love or are you simply filling your time with distractions? Are you honestly ready for a relationship or partnership or are you simply lonely and need a pet? Above all, before you can sing a duet with a partner, ask yourself can you dance to the beat of your own drum, or are you still trying to find your own beat? I'll be honest, finding my own tempo wasn't easy, in fact, sometimes it took dancing offbeat and looking crazy by observing the looks from people around me to change my ways.

Although we have our own sound, we have to be able to flow effortlessly with the people around us. We are all connected by one sound, and it wasn't until I began to realize the ups and downs in life were normal, and in order to flow, I had to enjoy my own rhythm and pay attention to creating my own sound. When you begin to be yourself and enjoy your quirks and originality, just like in a song, is when the tune changes, but every sound comes together perfectly and the song of life gets even better. It's when you are out of tune with reality is when you get lemons are thrown at you or pie. If you have never tried humble pie, count yourself as lucky and extremely rare. My first taste of humble pie was served on a shiny platter but wasn't appealing as you would think.

Life can come at you fast and sometimes when you aren't prepared, it can smack you in the face. When you get too accustomed to things going well, the things that can go the wrong start to become less of a common thought. Young and eager, I was so excited to be on my own at the age of nineteen. I was bright-eyed and bushy-tailed about setting out on my own. “Being an adult isn't as hard as they make it seem, this is easy”, I would think to myself as I graduated high school with a full-time managerial job and soon earned a government job with a good salary. Things seemed to be starting off really great for me as a young woman, and I thought that the good times would never end. We tend to think that when things are going well that they must be right for us. On what seemed like the worst day ever at the time, I was hit with the news that I would be let go just three months after I had moved into a new apartment and had no money saved.

At the young age of twenty, I was unaware and oblivious to the notion of saving for a rainy day so naturally, I looked to the people whom I called friends. It is not until things get real, that we realize who our true friends are. It was easy for me to get accustomed to my way of life and I had to learn the hard way that preparing for my future was a must. Jobs are temporary but true friendships are hard to come by. “Who are the people who will be by my side through the ups and downs when life throws curveballs and smacks me right in the face”, I asked myself. What we often forget is that life is constantly changing. What that means is that as people, and living organisms we are always growing and since we are all connected, we have to take care of the people we are in direct connection to.

In order to grow a relationship beyond friendship and build a real connection, communication is key. How we speak and treat one another creates a chain reaction in the lives of others that surround us. When we show up for others, there will be some that do not reciprocate when you need it, but it's also going to be times when people will show up for you. However, there is a lesson to be learned, that when we do for others, we cannot expect instant gratification of them returning what we would for them. We must be flexible with people and allow people to adjust themselves in their own time because we are all adjusting to the things that life throws at us. Friendship doesn't mean that their lives will revolve around you and you can pick them up whenever you need them. We must be flexible with people and allow people to adjust themselves in their own time. Think about it, if you were to only seek to receive that which you need in its perfect timing with no expectations of what it may look like, you would be surprised at what you find. You may be surprised to know that the things or people that you need do not come in the way that you thought it would appear. For instance, you may be looking for a quarter and would be surprised to find five nickels in your purse. Meaning what you are seeking in one person, is sometimes better suited in the form of five separate people serving one purpose.

Friendships are the backbone of your personal life because no matter what you go through, you can always count on your friends to have your back. Starting any relationship as a friendship has proven to be more beneficial in the long run. As I got older, I learned that when you allow things to flow effortlessly, that is when you can allow life to show you what you need, rather than what you think you want. As a teenager, I had no clue what I wanted out of relationships. I was just excited to have the freedom to explore my love life to figure out what love really meant to me. Even as a young woman in my twenties, the concept of love was still an idea to me and the reality of being in love was still very intriguing to me. We often hear about how to love someone else but not how to receive love. The one problem was that I was trying to fill a void that I knew nothing about. My concept of love was built on self-love and if someone doesn't love everything about you and caters to your every need then they do not love you. It wasn't until my late twenties that I learned that what I thought was the way to have romantic love wasn't what love really was. The notion that true love was nowhere to be found and there were no men qualified to receive, it became a thought of the past.

Growing up with a single mother, I was a hopeless romantic, praying that one day I would be a married woman, which naturally meant I would be in love and happy. I had once imagined love to be like what I would watch on television. Watching rom coms and "chick flicks' ' about finding "the one" made me truly believe in having the fairy tale ending but didn't have much to look up to in real life. With no example, and no Love Handbook, most people have to take a chance at love with their hearts on the line. No one tells you that when you enter into relationships, you are taking a gamble. Love once seemed like a happy place, a paradise, and something that was treasured and pure. As an adult in my thirties, my heart went through hard times because of my own inability to take care of my heart along the way.

My love began so pure and happy, I was eager to share my joy with others but I learned that it's important to believe that your heart is too valuable to share before you put it on the line of fire. What once was a paradise, soon became a task of walking through the fire and not getting burned. Before understanding this, I wore my heart on my sleeve and just a young girl with a heart of gold hoping to become a wife. My first try at love, or better yet, the first time I put my heart on the line, was the spring of 2008. I was a senior in highschool, and the song "Teenage Love Affair" by Alicia Keys was playing on repeat. What a time to be in love! If you aren't sure if you have ever been in love before, this is what it feels like when I fell in love with no parachute for the first time. All my time was spent thinking about my lover and I wanted to spend every waking moment with him. Blinded by love and not knowing what I wanted, allowed me to overlook red flags that I never would have known to look for at the time. At this point in my life, I had no clue this was something to worry about and would later turn into my deal breakers for future relationships. At the time, I could see only the best in that person and already be dreaming of our futures together. The reality was the future that I had planned alone in my head with little help from reality, was in fact just a dream. If you are in love for the first time or falling in love don't be alarmed if you are already picking out your wedding dress and naming your imaginary children. As you get to know the person more and more, you start to fall deeper and deeper into the love trance with every waking day, and eventually, you can't find a reason to leave them. Once you get to the point where nothing comes before them, you are there, you're in love. This can be a dangerous place to be if you aren't friends with the person first and sure of what you need for yourself to be happy alone. If you don't know what you actually want in life, love will only complicate your fears and cause self-sabotage and chaos. Once you have reached this stage of a relationship, strap on your seatbelt because it's going to be a bumpy ride as you navigate life with your partner. This is the stage of love outside of friendship and connection, you're smitten! Hold on tight, if you get too carried away in this stage without the right partner, you could make the mistake I made of putting too much on the line with no one to support you when the road gets tough. If you aren't careful or if you're anything like me, you can become addicted to the love drug.

Love can be good for you but it can also feel like a drug, it's a risk you take so it should be taken with caution. Sometimes what we think is love can be confused with obsession or lust. When you find your true love, you will know because it won't feel like they have a stronghold on you. Obsession is not love but it can feel like it when a person is struggling with codependency issues, feel the need to have a relationship to feel wanted, or have not mastered self-love yet. True love should feel more like freedom than control and flows effortlessly because you aren't acting out of fear and worry because it is truly yours. What belongs to you won't make you worry about it leaving and you won't want to leave because you will have everything that makes their day brighter. What a beautiful feeling to love someone and bring joy and happiness into someone's life! It can feel good to make someone's day brighter just by being a part of it.

When you are loving someone correctly you will feel like Ciara in "Can't Leave Em Alone" with 50 Cent in their 2006 single and no matter what anyone says you will be committed to your love. When you are sure that this is the right person to complement your sound, falling in love happens gracefully and naturally. However, I made the mistake of falling in love quickly and diving headfirst in. I threw all rational thinking to the wind and became so infatuated that I overlooked red flags in search of my perfect person. “No person is perfect. What is living without making some mistakes”, I would think to myself. Someone should have told me that “you can’t go looking for love” because I had no idea what I was looking for. What is love? Love is a burning fire that is sparked with the right connection. Love can set like wildfire when two people are devoted to spreading joy and happiness. I was tired of taking a backseat in my life, and always wondering what it would feel like when I knew what it felt like. What I was seeking was always within me. It wasn’t difficult for me to completely forget that I was the conductor of my own life and if I didn’t want to do something, I shouldn’t be confined to a life based on a relationship, I needed to free myself from the bondage of obsession and lust. When two people don’t mesh well, what was once a beautiful thing can turn very ugly.

Making a connection last takes care of both people to keep the sparks flying. Once one person stops putting in the effort to cultivate love, the train stops, and all passengers must get off. What happens when your partner on the love train jumps off-board before you are ready, it crashes. That was the outcome of rushing into a relationship without a real connection and before I had found the right person for me. When we learn that a person is not right for us, we have to leave because if we don’t they will escape, and you will be left with the damages. Even after I learned that this person was not right for me, what stopped me from leaving this Love Train? When all the things that I thought was true, was actually a facade built solely out of my own imagination. What was I truly seeking, someone to love, or someone that loved me? It’s common to confuse our need for self-love with our need to give love. There is nothing selfish about loving yourself and oftentimes the love you share with others is the love you need. It is when we feel offended that we do not receive the love we give in return is when we have to question what we really want in return? This directly aligns with the understanding that we all are different and in turn express ourselves in many ways. Before you can recognize if someone is loving you correctly, you should pay attention to the ways that you love yourself.

When you learn to embrace what makes you unique, the things that you may not appreciate, you may be surprised to find that there is someone out there that will show extra love to those parts of you. Allow someone to love everything about you, and to compliment you in ways that add to your life rather than takeaway. I discovered my own beauty when I took the time I needed to take care of myself inside and focused on becoming a better person. I stopped allowing people in my life that took my strengths for granted and exemplified by shortcomings. There was nothing to gain from a person that devalued me, especially when it comes to the person who I choose to be my life partner. Choosing a partner who does not see my worth as I do will in turn show me their own lack of valuing themselves. The person you choose as a partner is a reflection of yourself and the way they treat you plays a big part in how you treat yourself.

If you ever find yourself not loving yourself as much, pay close attention to the people you are loving and see if they are reciprocating love in any way. You can not pour from an empty cup so even if your partner is loving you correctly, it won't ever be enough if you are not loving yourself first. For so long, it was as if I was trying to fill a void that existed, and no matter how many love songs I listened to, I couldn't break the feeling that something was missing in my life. Growing as a young woman, I no longer yearned to fill this void with love and sex from the opposite sex. I replaced this desire to have a partner in love with the desire to have self-love and cater to myself in all ways that I wished for in a partner.

The desire to have something that was all mine, something that I could grow with while continuing to grow as a woman. I just couldn't pinpoint what it was until I had a revelation in my mid-twenties, in the words of the one and only Beyonce Knowles, "the best revenge is my paper".No more settling for less than what I deserved, and accepting less than greatness from myself. There was no more time for waiting for something to change without first changing myself. In 2016, I quit my full-time job to pursue my dreams and live my life on my own accord. There was nothing but time being wasted by expecting everyone to be in full support of my plans. Time was flying by fast and I realized that if I wanted more for myself, it was up to me to do what I had to do to make sure that made things happen. I packed my bags and traveled across the country to Las Vegas to start my business and get a fresh start. At the time, I was with a man that shared the same values as me and seemed to be a good partner on my business journey. Finding someone who shared my love for business, money, and success was a recipe for becoming a power couple and my yearning for love was awakened again. Having someone to push you and support your dreams is a blessing and to be able to do the same for someone else is a dream come true. Being an entrepreneur is not for the weak and is tough when you are in the beginning stages before you are established as a business owner.

For any relationship, it can be tough when making big life changes and being in uncharted territories. In turn, my relationship began to suffer, in part to me prioritizing my career goals over my love life. Years of pain in relationships created a guard that only the love of business could penetrate. My ex was a great guy and could have been a great match for me at a different point in my life. However, at that time, romantic love was replaced with my desire for succeeding and superseded any emotion because I knew that no matter what I always had something that would never leave me. For a woman in business, there has to be a balance of personal life and business and it can be difficult when those lines are blurred.

Learning to distinguish the difference between business partnerships and love partnership brought me to the understanding of the next stage of love: Partnerships. Outside of my business life and love of success, I am still a woman who wants to experience love from the right person. Learning that having a life partner is a part of my success allowed me to be more vulnerable and open to receiving what I want out of a man. Opening up my mind to accepting someone from a different walk of life has allowed me to recognize that there were parts of myself that I was neglecting. My need for a partner has become more important as I get older and have the desire to start a family and enter into the next level of my own life: Family. I have reached a point of success in my career that I am satisfied with and will continue to grow but the concept of having someone who appreciates those other parts of myself outside of my career is a blessing.

Once I realized that I wanted romantic love, it encouraged me to show those parts of myself more attention. Expressing my feelings became more important and being able to not allow my emotions to overwhelm me was a challenge. After holding back for so long, it was important that I took the time to care for myself. Lashing out in pain was only hurting me in the long run. Practicing self-care regularly is addicting but when someone does not care about you, you will be able to recognize it much easier than when you are neglecting yourself. Life is about teaching people how you want to be treated by example and if we show people that we are willing to neglect ourselves to cater to them, we are teaching people to put themselves before us. If you continue this pattern and continuously put people before yourself, and before you know it, you will realize how everyone has progressed.

While everyone else was making sure that they have what they need, and you weren't, your life is staying the same. Self-care is the cornerstone of having a healthy life and fostering healthy relationships. How you treat yourself is how life will treat you. Remember to take care of yourself, take care of your loved ones, and watch how God will take care of you!

Pretty WORTH IT

Samentha Moore

There I stood, staring straight into the mirror, recognizing an unrecognizable part of myself. How could I be here? A mash-up of feelings ranging from shame to pride enveloped me all at once. I took a deep breath as I stole one last look in the mirror, whispered "You're worth it, Sam." I said my last of what felt like my 1000th prayer of the day, turned off the lights, grabbed my keys, and headed out. I was driving to my future.

A little over nine years before that day, I was starting the rest of my life, when I got married at the age of 21. I was so thrilled to say, "I do." That is what I was raised to do, go to college, get a consistent job, get married, have kids...the works. When I was a little girl, I sometimes wondered what being a single adult woman would look and feel like, but growing up in a strict Haitian household, it was customary to live with parents until marriage. There was not much room to daydream about autonomy when the plan was already mapped out.

I never developed the confidence as a young girl to grow up with the world being my oyster, even with having an alpha personality. The lack of words of affirmation, over time, created a void that began to be filled with self-hate and self-doubt. Not feeling seen or heard in the most impressionable parts of my life created in me a people-pleasing nature, constantly doing for others to my own disadvantage because that is where I found tangible worth. Not understanding or realizing that I was the one who always held the key to my worth.

Between society hammering in my mind that I needed a man other than Christ to complete me, I patiently and excitedly awaited the day that I would flee from the strict rules of my childhood home and create a new one of my own with my husband and future kids. Focusing so much on this one goal was to my detriment, that should have been the time that I was developing my own self, finding my individual worth and identity, not waiting for it to be validated by someone else. Spinning with deeply cut wounds from my own father, who told me that "the moment you came out of your mother's womb, we never connected." My focus to find a man who did not say and do the things he did to my mother was key. I thought that would be good enough, right? He does not do these things, and he does these things, simple. No. There is an entire grey area, that is the area I wished I were guided more about.

I developed into a people pleaser, and so many factors contributed to that, from being the only black girl in my entire school to being the youngest child to living in a bi-cultural world. Those factors made it to where, unless someone said "good job" or "ok, go" I wasn't sure or confident in what to do, and unfortunately, those weren't words that I was exposed to near enough. That same mentality crept into my marriage. I look back and assess my dating season with my husband, there was a time early in our dating that he would not even hold my hand, or refer to me as his girlfriend! It was almost like he was embarrassed by me; I knew that was wrong, but I stayed. Because to me, finding someone who would agree to be with me was all I needed. The world would constantly tell me that I was beautiful, smart, and vivacious, yet, I decided to dwell in a space that was emotionally unavailable for me. The crazy part of not knowing your worth is your ability to withstand treacherous emotional storms.

My father would hammer Ephesians 22-24 into me and my sister's head about being a subservient wife, but he never cared to talk about

Ephesians 25-33 and dissect the entire verse that shows how the husband is charged to love his wife. The pressure to become a wife that worships her husband and never considers herself was palpable.

Ephesians 22-33

22 Wives, be subject to your own husbands, as to the Lord. 23 For the husband is the head of the wife, as Christ also is the head of the church, He Himself being the Savior of the body. 24 But as the church is subject to Christ, so also the wives ought to be to their husbands in everything.

25 Husbands, love your wives, just as Christ also loved the church and gave Himself up for her, 26 so that He might sanctify her, having cleansed her by the washing of water with the word, 27 that He might present to Himself the church in all her glory, having no spot or wrinkle or any such thing; but that she would be holy and blameless. 28 So husbands ought also to love their own wives as their own bodies. He who loves his own wife loves himself; 29 for no one ever hated his own flesh, but nourishes and cherishes it, just as Christ also does the church, 30 because we are members of His body. 31 For this reason a man shall leave his father and mother and shall be joined to his wife, and the two shall become one flesh. 32 This mystery is great; but I am speaking with reference to Christ and the church 33 Nevertheless, each individual among you also is to love his own wife even as himself, and the wife must see to it that she respects her husband.

Living a past of heavy abuse, my already stunted self-worth and lack of self-discovery led me to walk into any opportunity feeling like I was unworthy, even if it were my own skills and merit that got me there. The need to continually prove myself worthy became part of my self-identity. I knew deep inside that I was experiencing terrible treatment, but desperate to feel "chosen" in any capacity, I let it slide. As dating continued, he would say to me "I can't wait to watch you blossom." Honestly, that was it for me, hearing that made me really feel that I had someone that was choosing to love me for me now and the future me. Words and actions are on two different planets, I was so hungry for the words, that I chose to ignore the actions that I was often experiencing.

I did not have many family traditions growing up, and it seemed like the few things my family's generations were consistent with were unhealthy marriages. Watching my mother endure and live through a terrible marriage, I was determined to break that cycle, I was not getting a divorce, I was going to honor my commitment, even if it were to my detriment...again, focusing on what others thought of me. I failed to realize that my main commitment should have always been rooted in the commitment of and to myself.

Reeling from the effects of sexual abuse at the hands of strangers, my worth was compromised on every level. Who would want me? I was damaged and clearly, I was giving off an energy that made me deserve that treatment. Struggling with recovering within a household that was not groomed for open communication, my healing felt like it was once again, contingent on the approval of others. When I shared with my father that I was sexually assaulted, his response was, "I was held at gunpoint and robbed, and I got over it." I even heard the words, "what are people going to think of me because you keep getting sexually assaulted?" The cave that I created to emotionally retreat was so deep, at the time, I did not even realize it. This was when I first began to self soothe, internalizing everything, and not communicating or finding any healthy outlet. I did not want to be an emotional burden to anyone.

Prior to getting married, I asked my soon to be husband if my past of sexual assault would be an issue, so early into my healing, I was not quite sure what the future would look like. I did not want to live with someone resenting me over it, I could not bear to imaging that. I should have made the decision for my own life to take the time to heal. It should never have been a question or an option. That was not fair to either one of us. Patience being a virtue never rang truer for me than in that regard.

As the years went on, I quickly watched the excitement to watch me blossom shifted to verbal, mental, and emotional abuse. From telling me that I had not "earned" a wedding ring upgrade for a ring I was allergic to, to tell me in front of his father and sister, that he did not need to "respect" me, but to only love me, to saying that because of my past with sexual abuse, if he chose to step outside of the marriage, it would be warranted. Things escalated quickly, safety turned into feeling un-tethered, and I found myself, 26 years old, scared confused, and absolutely terrified that I had entered into a silent hell that I was going to have to die in order to get out of.

When I gave birth to my daughter, my lens began to refine. I remember being at the doctor's office waiting to hear the gender, I prayed for a boy, I thought to myself that if I had a boy, I could raise him to be the man that honors God. The truth was, I was terrified to have a girl because I did not think that I was worthy enough to rear a young lady in this world when I was struggling to be one myself. Her presence in my world was an automatic beacon of accountability. Now, I was the mother of a girl that I was going to have to teach her how she would need to teach others to treat her. It made me re-examine everything and everyone. The treatment that I was settling and accepting was hanging like a monkey on my back. Determined to still be the best wife, I figured being a great mom will turn the tides in my marriage, when he sees my commitment to our family, he will see that I am worth it.

Being active in church, we were always opening our home, we were completely forward-facing. Being such a young family, it became our reputation in the community. Not having many peer wives to open to and share, I suffered in silence. One evening, I had three girlfriends over for a last-minute dinner, we were all sitting around the table when my then husband said "I don't like the way Sam does her eyebrows." and proceeded to humiliate me in front of our guests. Not wanting to add to the already uncomfortable situation, I just made a light joke and kept it moving right along. Allowing this behavior to normalize in my marriage was something years down the road I had to take accountability for. He should have never spoken to me in that manner, especially in front of others, and I should have never allowed it.

As time went on, the disrespect and not being considered took a toll, falling into depression and self-loathing, wondering what I was doing wrong or what I did to deserve this. Maybe this was normal, is what I would say, growing pains. We completely stopped going on dates, something that was extremely important to me. Being a young family, finances were tight, so we did not always have the opportunity to do that, although, over time, funds were always found for other activities if needed. My mentality was that if I stuck through the growth and the hard seasons, that it would turn around for us, for me. Ride or die. Literally.

When we moved from Kentucky to DC, that was the beginning of the end for me. Uprooting your entire life and creating a new normal will really bring truths to light. The lack of maturity and consideration did not only hurt my feelings but also made him make poor decisions that at times, were life-threatening. My lifelong fear of having to live on my own and now not only have my mouth to feed, but my daughter became more and more of a reality.

Years of being controlled physically, mentally, spiritually, and financially wore me down to an inexplicable depression. One day, he came home from work and said to me, "you know, you are not anything to look at, when I come home from work, you need to be dressed nicer." That was a gut punch to me. Being a new mom, cooking, cleaning, and raising our daughter was lonely. My body issues were at an all-time high, I was sacrificing precious new mother sleep to wake up early and work out every morning because that is what he wanted. Being shamed for not being able to produce enough breast milk for our daughter after six months. On the other side of the same coin, I was not being able to so much as purchase a bra without permission or being told to wait until tax returns made me feel like I was a slave. Waking up early and cooking breakfast, lunch, and dinner daily, staying at home raising our sweet sweet sweet daughter. Feeling seen and beautiful was foreign to me, being told that I was basically ugly solidified exactly how I felt throughout my marriage. The crazy part was, he told me that he would take me shopping, and although I was hurt at the reason why he wanted to take me shopping, I was happy to go shopping, period. The lack of attention was so immense that even negative attention was desperately sought after.

The constant fear that what I was doing or who I was not enough, was slowly killing me, feeling unworthy and paranoid became muscle memory. No sleep, depression, anxiety were my daily vitamins. I knew that I was either going to have to leave this marriage and start my life over from scratch or die of a broken heart at age 30.

One day, I was meeting a friend for dinner. We lived in a seedy part of DC at the time. When I was finished getting dressed, I asked my ex to walk me out to the car, his response was that he was too tired. That made me feel less than a priority and that my safety wasn't even a factor. I was filled with anxiety all evening at dinner, because I knew that this was something that I needed to speak up about, for myself. When I got home, I confronted him about what happened earlier that evening and his response was "maybe you need to wear gym clothes on your way to the car and change when you get to your destination." When I pushed back on his response, I was returned with a "you're acting like a bitch." This made things clear to me that I was not considered in my own life. That my wellbeing was not a factor. What do you do when you come to this realization?

Much like someone who has suffered from pica, I was in a place of so much lack for so long, I craved any type of attention, period. Negative, positive, or indifferent. The lack of positive reinforcement over the years caused me to think that I did not need it and that I was strong because of it. I walked through my life carrying hurt and pain from myself and from others, convincing myself that it was easier for me to absorb the pain instead of addressing it head-on. A lack of self-worth will make you believe that what you have to say is not important.

I never took a moment to look inside of myself and consider that accepting and enduring a lack of healthy love and positive affirmation had me built up walls that were sky high. It is a full-time job to act like everything is together when you are in public but behind closed doors suffer in silence. It is exhaustive in many ways, and you cannot fool everyone. As time went on, those closest to me started to see and experience things themselves. This made me angry because I did not want anyone to think that my life was crumbling, it was embarrassing and incredibly difficult to accept. I had two friends approach me on separate occasions asking me if everything was ok. I lashed out in anger. One friend said to me "this doesn't look like what a healthy marriage should be." I internalized that as an automatic failure on my part, instead of seeing that as someone who was looking out for me and my best interest. As time progressed, I had to be held accountable for the reality that I was living in and started to open to those closest to me about my experiences.

Things heightened to the point that we were not sleeping in the same bed, much less the same room and our schedules reflected that of shift workers, one coming home in time to relieve the other one to leave. The less time we spent together, the less arguing and the better for us all. One day I was cleaning our bedroom and I saw a journal that he had been writing in, desperate for answers, I flipped through the pages of his journal and staring at me was the truth that I was feeling but not told all along. One entry talked about how for years, I was told that I was "fake" when in truth, he admitted that he lived in jealousy towards me because people were so quickly drawn to me. As painful as the words were to read, it helped me to see exactly what I needed to do. Although I had countless instances and experiences to stand on, being able to visually read how someone felt about me, an energy I was feeling for an insufferable amount of time brought me some clarity and comfort. I was not crazy after all. It boggled my mind that there would be such competition within a union that is supposed to be a team effort. My thought process was always "if you win, or I win, we win", so to live in an atmosphere that was the complete opposite, is draining in every way.

The only way that I was able to feel safe communicating was by writing. By writing a letter, I was able to be clear, honest, and not get cut down for every emotion that I had. I had more courage with a pen. I had letters dated back for years, as early as our first year of marriage. They all ended with the same sentiment, that I would no longer tolerate control and disrespect, except I was and did...until I did not. I wrote what was to be my last letter of this nature. Expressing the lack of thought and consideration I received yet the expectation of respect of and intimacy that he had for me to give, I could no longer do. Looking back on the years that I was silenced and left to self soothe. Like a salamander, I would lose a limb and hide off to regenerate somewhere, the same cave my own father put me in. Alone. The final letter I wrote was found with markings all over it, markings that ranged from criticizing my weight, saying no more effort would be given, to outright saying "fuck you" and calling me an "asshole jerk". I remember trying to sneak out of the house before he read the letter, I wanted to ensure some time and space to digest things. I was too late, with my hand on the doorknob, I was met with a rage that resulted in me being physically pushed out of my own home, the front doorknob being broken, with my 3-year-old screaming for me and being told "your mother is a monster". That is when I was sure, I had to leave at whatever cost. I remember getting in to the car of my best friend and uncontrollably sobbing. I called my mom, blurting everything I could muster up through my tears. I stayed in that car, for what felt like a lifetime, staring at the door that I was just pushed out of, wondering how I could ever go back in? Not after that blow out. I went back in, defeated and scared. My then husband knocked on the door of the room I was sleeping in and asked me, “Are you thirsty? Do you need anything?” I was floored. Didn’t we both just experience the same terror just hours ago? No other moment than that made me realize there was absolutely no reasoning or salvagin what was going on. My own judgement was completely compromised and impaired. Gaslighting at its finest.

Even though I was suffering years in silence, I was always told to protect my husband and my marriage. I wish that someone added, above all else, protect yourself. The fear of judgment superseded my need for completeness. Being raised in the church, you hear regularly how much God hates divorce, I understood that then and I still do now. Ultimately, God wants us to live a life that pleases and serves Him, if within a marriage I cannot do or be that, that is a sin to me. To not be able to live or love in purpose, is greater than sacrificing your entire life just to stay married. We stayed separated for three years, it took me that long to come to the decision that divorce was the best course of action. It took me three years to get over the fear of what others thought and to start living life between me and God. It took me getting ex-communicated from the church that I was a part of to realize just how hypocritical and apathetic those who should love the most can be. I stopped looking to the Bible to see what it said about divorce and started looking to the Bible to see what is said about marriage. Big difference. To this day, when my daughter asks why we got divorced, I simply tell her "our marriage was not one that was honoring the Lord, and the purpose He created me for".

I pulled up to the parking lot at church, my heart was in my throat and my stomach felt like it had bottomed out. I knew that this was the meeting that I was going to sit down and tell my husband that when he came back from his work trip abroad, that I would not be there. I knew this man since I was 17 years old, I had no idea what being alone truly meant. I had a toxic dependency on the faux support that I lived with for a decade, but it turned into a matter of life and death for me. I was at the point of no return, not a penny to my name, not a job, not even a completed Bachelor's Degree, I was ready to step into the world a create my own safe space for me and my daughter. I decided that I would rather suffer and struggle by myself than endure the intimate hatred I had to live in day to day.

The separation was not easy, I tried to go against everything society said separation would look and feel like. Eleven months of marital counseling seemed to do more harm than good. All I wanted was my freedom, nothing else. I found an apartment and signed for it with no job and no car, just prayers, and a determination to make it. I found a temporary job that would help me pay bills for my daughter, and I leaned on the support of family and close friends to support and pray for me. The entire season was painful in every way, physically, mentally, spiritually, financially, and emotionally.

Having to sit within me was one of the hardest things I ever did. To accept loneliness in its entirety is painful, it hurts emotionally and physically. To make the intentional choice to begin the work of peeling back layers that have been avoided for generations. Having to get to know and cater to my own broken inner child. I do not think I had a night where I did not cry myself to sleep. Happy for my newfound freedom, and terrified of the unknown. The years of being told I was nothing arriving front and center in my mind, every waking moment. Carrying a backload of anger that could move mountains. Mourning a lifetime that will no longer happen, hopeful for a future that will. Peeling myself out of bed just to do the bare minimum and staying in it all day and all night when I had the chance, all while putting on a smile for a child that is looking up to you. There is nothing relaxing or cute about healing, it is ugly and grueling. But to choose yourself is the greatest act one can do not only for yourself but the world around you.

In my newfound quiet moments, I would sit in my apartment and just look around, even if I was hurting, there was a part of me that was always able to take a deeper breath than I was able to in over a decade. No money in the bank was ok with me, because at least I had my freedom, and that was everything. Being able to create a healthy and safe atmosphere for myself and my daughter was absolutely everything. The opportunities that God afforded me was mind-blowing, opportunities that I know I would have never thought I was worth or could even accept in my previous life. Even though I was 31 years old, I felt like I was a teenager, starting life for the first time on my own.

Self-care became the newest trend in the world, but it was a lifeline for me. Finding forgiveness opportunities starting with myself and working my way through the list. Creating healthy boundaries and having hard conversations with many in my life. Letting go of some relationships that were triggering and intentionally seeking others that were edifying. Meditating daily and speaking positive affirmations to myself, finding communities that helped me in these ways. Stepping outside of the girl that I lost years ago, holding her hand, and stepping into the woman I am today.

Through therapy, a newfound and steadfast connection to Christ, I learned that no one could control me. People are put in place that can take advantage of a situation, but ultimately the control factor lies within the mentality. The lack of self-discovery and self-worth. Even the most beautiful person aesthetically in the world can feel a lack of worth because worth is the canvas that we are built on. The absence of painting that canvas does not keep it clean, something will always paint onto it, that could be positive, or negative. As women, we put ourselves on the back burner, in every way, and that is if we even put ourselves on a burner, to begin with. Your identity, presence, and worth are not contingent on how well you cook a meal, how cute you dress, or how well you can clean a house. We are more than executing tasks and caring for others. We are multi-dimensional beings and it is up to us to teach others how to treat us.

To allow and watch yourself blossom from where you were to where you are now is an experience that every woman is entitled to experience. No one can tell you whether you can do it or how to navigate it. One of the greatest superpowers a woman has is her intuition, that is why the world tries to take it and challenge it so much. You push yourself in ways that you would never have, even in the false safety and guise of a broken relationship. Individual identity is worth more than the sum of two broken souls. Loneliness, depression, disrespect, and crawling through the emotional trenches is incredibly difficult, but that is where you find the glow. The glow doesn't come from makeup, or how skinny you are, or what you are wearing, that glow is the work of a woman who knows what she has been through and doesn't need anyone to validate her, the glow comes from the healed parts of you within, the glow comes from the still broken parts of you that you choose to acknowledge. Being in a place where you are and know yourself, what you want and need, and where you are going is pretty worth it.

Pretty STRONG
Natima Sheree

Experience + Self-Awareness – Pride = Strength

I use to hate the phrase "what doesn't kill you makes you stronger," because my translation of that statement was "if the tragedy or trauma, doesn't physically kill you, then the emotional state it leaves you in, will make you feel like you wanna die." I struggled with this theory. Like, who proudly affirms this mantra? You're telling me the only way to develop strength is to damn near die in the process? I just couldn't accept this, so I decided to change the phrase to "what doesn't kill you, wasn't supposed to!" Period! I learned very young that strength is a choice, not a default action or reaction. Strength is a state of mind and an emotional posture. It is not something you catch or inherit. It's developed, it's built, and it's earned!

Since I was a child I was always recognized as the *strong* one. Physical strength, not so much, my younger sister Trina got most of that; but emotionally, mentally, and spiritually, I was a giant! This quality was developed and recognized at birth. Since the womb, I've been a fighter! Born premature at just 29 weeks, my parents knew I was strong. At just 3 lbs. and 7 oz. I was determined to live and was breathing on my own after just several hours outside the womb. God already had plans for my life and developing my strength would be a key component to my purpose. I knew it, my parents knew it and it was a matter of time before the world would come to know it. Strength became the standard of my life. Everything I faced, everything I experienced I responded in strength and used challenges and trails as strength builders. Growing up, I dealt with bullies, insecurity, my parents' divorce, homelessness, brokenness and abuse, and it was my strength that got me through.

For me, strength was innate. It was threaded into the fiber of my being, an intrinsic skill that I had developed, and damn near mastered. I didn't always value my strength or appreciate it because I assumed strength was something we all had. However, after observing mental breakdowns, drug addiction, and alcohol abuse that consumed lives, destroyed families and careers, and devastated communities, I realized just how wrong I was to assume we all possess the same level of strength. By no means am I judging anyone as our journeys and stories are unique, however, witnessing devastation and hardship made me appreciate my own strength and ability to deal, to heal, and to overcome circumstances and unfavorable situations that have destroyed, or broken the average person. Because of this, I knew I wasn't average.

What I once took for granted, I have grown to appreciate, love, and leverage daily. I'm so confident in my strength that I'm borderline conceited about it. I brag on my strength! I know it's nothing but strength and maturity that keeps me from posting certain shit on social media, responding to a hater or even allowing someone to pull me out of character. Its strength that keeps me from reverting to old ways, keeps me from giving up and keeps me from conforming to social norms or crumbling under the weight of negative cultural influences. Strength is a contributor to my uniqueness and my individuality. It's the foundation of my self-esteem, self-worth, and confidence. Strength is the force behind my "go-getter" attitude; and works in harmony with my motivation, purpose, and goal-driven mentality. It's what helps me to keep my head up, to stay focused and determined. I'm a strong MUTHA******* and am so glad I've reached this level in my life journey. Strength is the key ingredient in my life's success formula!

Strong Enough to Leave

At just twenty-two years old and barely out of undergrad I went from cap and gown to wedding gown in four months. Strong-minded and strong-willed, I was convinced that I was "in love" and ready for marriage. I was ready and willing to make the sacrifices to be a wife and to show my parents and peers that I was an adult and capable of standing on my own. A sad reality that wouldn't be revealed until years later, was that my husband and I were ill-prepared for marriage. Neither of us had grown up with examples of healthy marriages, had no true foundation, nor did we know who we were as individuals, which was necessity in building a strong, sustainable, and cohesive marriage. Nevertheless, on July 24, 2004, I took on a new last name, a new husband, and a new address clear across the country leaving my friends, family, and the only "home" I had ever known behind.

I remember sitting on the plane next to my husband, proudly clutching his arm and thinking to myself "I got this! I'm strong, I can do this!" Sadly I had no friggin clue what I was walking into or what was in store for me. Looking back, I didn't have the life skills, the experience, maturity, resilience, agility or mindset to be a wife or to live thousands of miles away from my family. I had no safety net, no network, no community, and no village. It was me, this man and the military.

It didn't take long for me and my husband's true colors to show. We were fighting constantly and didn't have the essential tools to work through our problems like adults. We'd do petty hurtful things to one another and chalk it up to inexperience. We'd fight, disrespect one another and then bandage the wounds with sex. No intimacy, no communication but emotionless, detached intercourse. I convinced myself this was how you deal with trouble in a marriage and didn't require, expect, or demand more. I never considered healing through communication, or counseling. I didn't even know it was an option. I was young and just assumed sex fixed everything. Little did I know, all

I was doing was digging a deeper hole for me, my marriage, my emotions, my self-esteem, and my affection to later be buried in.

As the years went on we grew further and further apart, we talked only when necessary and had mastered the "our marriage is perfect" front for friends, and family. We even had the nerve to be members of the marriage ministry at our church (the audacity right?). We had a brand new house, a vacation home, money in the bank, luxury vehicles, progressing careers, and a phony ass marriage. By year four we didn't even like each other, we simply tolerated one another. I just couldn't give up though, I thought staying and working hard to turn things around was what strong women did. I thought what I wanted didn't matter in marriage, that I had to do whatever it took to make my marriage last even at the expense of my own happiness. I just couldn't disappoint my family, my friends, or God with divorce. I was taught that divorce is the only judgment that has ever broken a covenant between man and God. The covenant of marriage and my promise to God was important to me and so I was willing to forfeit everything to save my marriage.

Convinced I was doing the right thing, we decided to have a baby, I just knew having a baby, and building a family would help to restore our relationship. I quickly learned just how wrong I was; as I gained weight from the pregnancy my husband became that much more unattracted to me. We slept in separate rooms and barely touched, talked or spent any time together. I was miserable and I know he was too but we just didn't know how to fix things. Our baby girl was born and that improved things for a while. We worked very well together as parents and got along perfectly when it came to her. Eventually our beautiful baby girl's presence only magnified the discord and dissension between us. My husband was an excellent father and co-parent and I loved him for it, but I realized having the baby gave us both an excuse to focus more on parenting and less on fixing our marriage.

As I prepared for my daughters' 2nd birthday party I remember thinking to myself, would I want my daughter to be in a marriage like this one? Could I do this for another sixteen years for her? Could I stay married to her dad just to give her the stability and security of a family? If I knew then what I know now, leaving would have been much easier and would have happened much sooner. Children witnessing their parent's happiness is just as important as seeing them in a fulfilling relationship. For decades, in my family, couples have stayed married for the sake of the children and were miserable, and their children knew it. I wanted to set a better example for my daughter. I wanted her to know that even if your marriage fails, there is love after divorce. I wanted her to see me happy and fulfilled even if that meant her Dad and I were no longer together. After lots of prayer, introspection, and time, I finally decided to end my marriage. As scared and unsure as I was about my future I knew it was the right decision. The transition was extremely hard for both of us but we figured it out and became better versions of ourselves which made us even better co-parents for our daughter. I have no regrets and gained a friend in my ex-husband. Our co-parenting isn't perfect, but it's healthier than our marriage was and my daughter is better because of our decision.

There is strength in leaving a situation, relationship, and even a career that no longer serves you. Too often we attribute or recognize our strength in our ability to stay and endure in a negative situation, but that to me is a false positive and misplaced strength. Just because you can carry a heavy burden doesn't mean you should or are supposed to. I found strength in my independence; I found strength in my vulnerability; and I found strength in starting over!

I'd rather be Strong than Stupid!

After my divorce, I stayed single for a while. I was inundated with life and had no time for a man. I had moved into a small townhouse and focused on building a new norm and a home for me and my daughter. Starting over was hard and required all my strength, focus, and time. I spent several years healing and finding myself, mastering motherhood, and falling in love with me again. I wasn't a single mother because my ex-husband was very present and engaged in our daughters' life, however, I was a single woman with a child, so dating was going to be very different, and I didn't want to rush into anything. I was still learning and discovering this new version of me! I had to figure out what I liked, what I didn't like, and was intentional in setting boundaries and waiting for what I wanted. My marriage had defined me and gave me my identity for so long, I was literally recreating myself and that took time and consistent effort.

After almost two and a half years I was finally ready for an active social life and even considered dating. I had lost weight, cut my hair, and redirected my focus toward personal goals, my purpose, and growing my career. I had spent time traveling, getting closer to family, finding new friends, and just doing things I liked. I felt like I had established balance as a professional, as a mother, and as a single woman. I was ready to meet someone who would complement what I had been able to build and establish for myself.

I decided to attend a Black Lives Matter event in Washington, D.C during the height of the movement following the deaths of Michael Brown and Eric Garner. I was interested in getting involved and supporting the D.C chapter of the organization, so this event was a great way to get in the mix. I loved the energy in the room and found myself mingling and networking with some of D.C's top social influencers and community leaders at the time. We had several speakers hit the podium that evening, but one in particular really stood out to me. He was very attractive, intelligent, and a well-known and respected young attorney. I laughed to myself as I heard the commentary of the women surrounding me; they weren't at all shy or coy in vocalizing their attraction to the event's final speaker. I can't lie, the man was fine. He stood about 6' 2", slim fit with great lips and nice eyes. I was definitely checking him out but wasn't about to openly admit it like some of the other women in the room.

When he stepped down from his address the women swarmed him. I knew there was no way I was getting to him, not even to compliment his speech; so I headed to the bar to take advantage of the free drinks before the event ended instead. I started chatting with another young attorney who was also taking advantage of the open bar. We chatted only briefly before being interrupted; to my surprise, it was the handsome speaker who I assumed would have been inundated with "fans." I remember turning around to see him standing there; my physical reaction was poised but on the inside, I was screaming "damn! You are too fine!" He spoke first and had the nerve to call me rude! "Rude?! How am I rude?" I asked. He smiled and said "because you walked away while I was still speaking." Knowing this wasn't true I just played along and told him "but I heard every word you said!" I was more flattered by the fact that he even noticed me in a room full of beautiful and successful women, that I didn't pick up on his condescending disposition. That should have been a red flag, but I paid it no mind. We flirted a bit longer before he finally asked for my number. Not completely ready for a man having that type of access to me, I offered my social media handles instead. He was appalled! I guess he wasn't use to a woman who didn't fall over him or sweat him, but I could tell he liked my tenacity, even though he probably wasn't used to it.

We communicated for several months via social media. We flirted, sent memes, and played twenty questions. I enjoyed the pace and felt comfortable with him. We had built a solid friendship and connection from the extensive correspondence and I felt he was genuinely interested in me as a person.

We finally moved the conversation off social media and began texting and talking. It was almost three months before we finally agreed to link. I invited him over for lunch since I worked from home full-time and I knew he had to be at court in my area that week. He came over and we literally spent five hours talking. NOTHING else, just talking and I loved it. I even missed scheduled conference calls that day because I just couldn't pull away. Our vibe was so genuine, our connection was dope… I was smitten. I was feeling this man and wanted to spend more time getting to know him. I knew, however, that there was still some insecurity I was battling because every time he complimented me I questioned his sincerity, I questioned if he really meant it. I couldn't accept that a man this attractive, this successful was actually interested in me. I heard someone say "that you date at the level of your self-esteem;" that statement couldn't have been more applicable and real for me. Nevertheless, I decided to ignore my apprehension and "let him in." I stopped putting up walls and stopped sending mixed signals. I opened myself up emotionally, mentally, and physically. Things were going well until they weren't and I immediately blamed myself. I was dealing with his lies, cheating, and him "needing to do him" and yet somehow in my mind, it was all my fault.

We were together less than a year when I found out I was pregnant. I literally didn't think I could take on any more bad or unpleasant news because of all I was already dealing with. I had just lost my younger sister and now had to decide if I wanted to have a baby with a man I've only been dating for about a year. This would have all been new to me! I had my first daughter in wedlock; I didn't have a "baby-daddy" but rather an ex-husband. I hated the thought of having a baby with a man I wasn't married to and just knew our relationship was not headed in that direction at all. Several months into the relationship I had learned that I was "sharing" my man with other women. One of which was bold enough to call my phone and tell me she doesn't mind sharing him since he already made it clear that he wasn't leaving me to be with her (the audacity right?). I had forgiven him for a lot in the beginning but his shenanigans were getting old. Here I was mourning the sudden death of my younger sister, trying to figure out what to do about my pregnancy, and now having to find out and confront him about his infidelity yet again! I was over it! It was all too much! I stayed in bed for days. No work. No food. No phone. Just tears and sleep. I didn't want to face any of my problems, especially not the issues in our relationship. After several weeks of ignoring his calls and texts, I finally agreed to see him and talk. In the most arrogant and detached way, he admitted to cheating… again! He attempted to comfort me by saying "but they know you're the one I'm with, you're the one I love." I swear I wanted to knock his head off his f*&#@! shoulders, but instead I laughed. I finally told him I was pregnant and was still deciding if I wanted to proceed with the pregnancy or not. He then laughed and asked if I was actually pregnant or just saying that to keep him. And yet again, the desire to knock the f$%#! out of him consumed my thoughts. One thing I learned early in life is that cheating is a choice! Men have no problem staying faithful to their favorite football team or basketball team, they have no issues being loyal to their barber, even when they have to wait hours for a cut… so it's definitely a choice to cheat on their lady. A part of me felt like I was wrong for taking him back after he cheated earlier in the relationship. I felt like I set a standard for disrespect. I know a lot of it was because of my insecurity and desire to be with someone like him. Nevertheless, that is never an excuse to stay with someone who doesn't respect, appreciate, or value you. I had to be strong enough to love myself and not accept his disrespect any longer. He was dope on paper, yes, but hell so was I! I brought just as much to the relationship and deserved better. Dealing with infidelity, disrespect, and cheating is not strength, it's settling. No woman deserves to be lied to, cheated on, or taken advantage of. I believe there are some men who mistakenly cheat, and then there are those men who are just cheaters. And he was indeed the latter.

Unsure of what to do I turned to my parents for counsel and advice. My parents are dope! They've made their mistakes, have their issues, but all and all are good people! I admired and respected their parenting style and have always observed their counsel and instruction. My parents are both very spiritual, centered and self-aware, (notice I said spiritual and not religious…) and so their opinions mean a lot to me. My parents had the same advice for me, keep the baby. They are firm believers in the circle of life and didn't view it as a coincidence that I became pregnant just weeks after losing my sister. Conflicted I just couldn't decide what to do, so I decided to see how *he* felt about our options. Keep the baby or terminate the pregnancy? Very nonchalantly he confirmed that he had no opinion in the matter, that it is my body and he will support whatever decision I made. After several more days of contemplating I decided to keep the baby and somehow he interpreted that as we would we be getting back together. But that was not the plan at all! I was convinced we could co-parent and not have to be romantically involved. There was no way I was going to be with a man that couldn't be faithful just because I was carrying his child. The best apology is changed behavior and it was clear he wasn't ready to change. The mistake I made in my marriage would not be made again. I was not about to compromise for any relationship what I didn't to save a marriage... my happiness and peace was non-negotiable.

Mommy Strength

I gave birth to a beautiful baby girl and did it alone. When I told my ex that we would not be getting back together just because I was pregnant, was literally the last time I saw him. He would reach out sporadically to ask about the pregnancy but wasn't present, supportive, or engaged in any way. Not financially, emotionally, or mentally. I had done everything alone. Attended every doctor visit alone. Decorated the nursery alone. Celebrated at my baby shower alone. And delivered my healthy baby girl and named her alone. It wasn't that he wasn't welcomed or invited to be a part but rather that he chose not to be. I don't know if ending the relationship despite the pregnancy bruised his ego or hurt his pride but it was unfair to take it out on our daughter. I remember being asked if I kept the baby in an attempt to trap him… I laughed and simply said "this man is not my meal ticket or my come up! This baby is a shared responsibility, not a level up opportunity for me." To this day he is not involved; however, instead of focusing on that, I just focus on being what my daughter needs. My reason for keeping my daughter was never about him and me but more so about what my parents said regarding the circle of life and my sister's passing. That resonated with me and really convicted me. To have just lost someone I loved so much and then to take another life for convenience, was a decision I just couldn't live with. Choosing to keep my daughter was not an easy choice but it was MY choice to make. And I'm living with the outcome resulting from that choice every day.

The first few months were really hard. Trying to be a mother to my nine-year-old, care for my newborn, and fight my battle with post-partum depression was hell. I cried daily, slept never, and was exhausted most of the time. I had occasional help but was mostly doing it on my own. I was juggling a career, two girls, a mortgage, a graduate degree, and personal goals. I was struggling to balance it all and was feeling anxious, defeated, and alone. I refused, however, to take the "woe is me" road. I was not about to complain and act like I'm the only woman going through it. If I've learned anything, I've learned that God has grace for single mothers. I've watched single mothers do amazing things for themselves and their children, so I knew I needed to just tap into that strength and push. I've witnessed single mothers work several jobs to provide for their families and send their kids to college. I've seen single mothers hold families together after their husband died or simply walked out. I've heard stories of single mothers working all day, attending school at night, and making it home to kiss their babies goodnight. I wish I would try to complain about a plight that is common to many. I believed this was just yet another opportunity to develop my strength and glow up!

I knew from birth Amiyah was special, after all, she possessed the same proven strength at birth that I had. However, even with my discernment and intuition, I wasn't ready for the bomb the doctor was about to drop on me. What I assumed was just a routine checkup, turned out to be a pivotal and defining moment for us both. My baby girl was diagnosed with Asperger syndrome! I felt the warm tears fall down my face as I sat with Amiyah on my lap. I immediately started to blame myself, not realizing at the moment, there was nothing I could have done, and nothing I could have kept her from that would have avoided this. The news hurt to my core and I just couldn't understand how this happened or truly what the diagnosis even meant. I was devastated and thought to myself "here is yet another thing I will have to face alone!" However, after days of crying and complaining, that voice inside me said "pull yourself together Sis! Wipe those tears and woman up! Your daughter needs to see your strength and power, not your sadness and pity!" I remember checking the time on my phone, it was 3:21 AM on Wednesday, August 21, 2019. I grabbed my laptop and began my research. I needed to first understand her condition and then create a plan on how to care for and support her. I knew exactly what I needed to do and who I needed to be for her. One year and three notebooks full of research notes later, I am managing my baby girl's "uniqueness." I am careful of the labels I place on her and dismissive of the ones that society tries to place on her and people like her. I have my days where single motherhood gets the best of me, but I hit that reset button as often as needed. I have to be strong for her! And although she's the only one who can see my cape, she's proud that her Mommy is her superhero and can't a damn thing stop that. I am her strength, her rock, and her safe place… Always!

Strong Holds That Hinder Your Focus

After my relationship with Amiyah's father ended it left me broken, insecure, and angry. I hated the situation, his absence from her life, and regretted some of the choices I had made leading up to that point. Personally, I felt unattractive, undesired, and unloved. I had hit a low place, emotionally, and felt empty inside. I needed a lift, a change, a reset, and a fresh start. I decided to turn things around for myself. I joined an online group that offered a 24-month self-love journey challenge and it was truly one of the best things I had ever done. I loved it! It was inspiring, informative, encouraging, motivating, and exactly what I needed. I was so dedicated and focused on my journey that I didn't realize I was a year and a half through the program when I met the man that would later become my boyfriend.

Regular exercise and workouts were a part of the journey requirements and expectations. It was a holistic program and dealt with the mind, body, and spirit. I remember leaving the gym feeling great about my workout and lost in my own positive energy that I didn't even see the man walking toward me. I walked right into the tall, chocolate handsome bearded man. Before I could speak, he smiled and said hello. I apologized quickly and kept it moving; because when you're focused on yourself, you literally don't see anything or anyone else, unless you want to, and at that moment, I did not see him!

Several weeks went by before I saw the young man again. I could tell he was younger than me but I didn't know exactly how much younger. I mean don't get me wrong, he was a grown-ass man, but definitely younger than me, so you can imagine how flattered I was when he asked me out. We went out for several months before we were intimate. I wanted to finish my self-love journey before sexually engaging with anyone and he respected this decision. Before becoming intimate, he admitted that he was dating several women and was willing to cut them off to enter an exclusive relationship with me, if and when I was ready.

Our relationship evolved quickly and we were fast friends and lovers. I loved our friendship most and really valued our connection. It wasn't long however before my intuition kicked in and my gut was telling me that he wasn't faithful. I hated to assume things based on feeling alone but I am not the type of woman who goes through a man's phone or social media account. I care but I be damn if I ever make those moves; I'd leave before I do all that. Instead, I flat out asked, are you cheating? Do I need to be concerned about your relationship with your daughter's mother? I admit I was STILL working through insecurity that I had been carrying for years. Insecurities that became heavier and more overwhelming after every failed relationship. So I decided to give him the benefit of the doubt and took him at his word when he told me he wasn't cheating and I had nothing to worry about.

Despite what he may have said, my intuition was still ringing the alarm! I still had this feeling in my gut that told me he was lying and that he was cheating too! Let me tell you something... One thing I know about my intuition, is that Sis ain't never wrong! Every time I've had a 'feeling' something was off, it was off! My gut ain't never lied to me! She might embarrass me by hanging over my pants a little or stick out too far in a photo, but Sis has never steered me wrong!

Several months after confronting my boyfriend, in the heat of an argument, he admitted that he not only cheated on me with his daughter's mother but that she was pregnant by him again! I immediately shut up and sat on the edge of the bed. My heart sank, and my body became hot. I felt numb and overwhelmed by conflicting emotions. I couldn't speak. I wasn't shocked or surprised, but more so disappointed. Disappointed in myself! I knew it and should have trusted my intuition months ago. Why was I so quick to believe these men but not myself? I was so hurt and felt so disrespected.

The problem was, I had spent two years doing all this inner work and building myself up but hadn't cut the ties and strongholds from prior relationships. I hadn't dealt with what had hurt me in my past. I hadn't let go of my baggage. I hadn't healed the wounds, I bandaged them. Every relationship I've had up to this point in my life has taught me something but had also taken a part of me. Yes, I grew stronger but I was hurt or broken first. I had to rebuild and pull myself from a low place every time. I learned from my failed relationships that there is no condom for the soul. You can't protect your spirit from the energy and vibration passed onto you or exchanged during intimacy or intercourse. There is no way to shield or protect your heart once you've been "naked," transparent, and vulnerable with someone you trust.

People hate to admit it, myself included, but there are things that we carry from relationship to relationship because we don't know how to let those parts and pieces of ourselves go. We hold onto who we were in those relationships not realizing we do more damage when we drag our old selves into new places. Letting the relationship go is but one part of the transition. We also have to let the hurt and broken pieces of us go too. You can't grow from dead roots. Everything that is no longer serving you or giving you "life" has to go.

It takes strength to walk away, and even more strength to heal. I've learned to go through things, and not around them. Even those unpleasant experiences deserve strength!

HER-cules

If you've gotten anything from my chapter and this small part of my story I hope you understand that strength is subjective. Strength is necessary for character building, integrity sustaining, faith enhancing and hope maintaining. Strength is armor, it's an invisible body guard and a constant partner.

Strength is holding it together for your children when everything in you is falling apart. Strength is wanting so bad to give up or give in but creating reasons not to! Its' getting knocked down and choosing not to stay down. Experiencing moments of weakness but not allowing those moments to define you. Strength is biting your tongue instead of responding to shade or negative rumors about you. It's wanting to be revengeful but choosing to be empathetic instead. Strength is choosing not to hurt those who have hurt you but forgive and move forward. Strength is knowing when to let go and when to hold on. Strength is defiant, it's bold, and it doesn't take no for an answer. Strength is pushy and bossy, it's inconsiderate at times and very demanding! Strength doesn't ask how you feel or if you're in the mood, it doesn't check your energy or care about the level you're vibrating. Strength expects a lot and requires even more. Strength is resilient and aggressive; it doesn't wait for an invite and doesn't ask for your permission. Strength is creating and enforcing boundaries and not allowing yourself to be mistreated for the sake of a relationship or friendship. Strength is knowing when to walk away from people and situations that no longer serve you. Strength is loving and respecting yourself in a shallow and superficial culture that tells you being your authentic self is not good enough.

Know that you are strong! No matter what you've been through, no matter what trauma and tragedy you've overcome, the fact that you are still here, still living, still breathing is proof that you have strength!

Your ability to overcome and excel, thrive, or just keep going takes strength. Sometimes just getting out of bed and facing another day takes an incredible amount of strength. Your setbacks, failures, challenges, and disappointments are more defining than you know. Learn to build your strength upon those experiences, don't be buried by them. I've learned that the strongest people aren't those who flex in front of others, but rather those who overcome challenges people don't even know that they've been facing!

May strength and dope vibes transform you!

From a *Pretty* Mess to a *Pretty* Messenger

Adunni Afolabi

Growing up I was often categorized as pretty. My outer description was light-skinned, long hair, pink lips with a slim build. But inside my description was anything but cute. Internally, I struggled with low self-esteem and low self-worth. I was insecure, fearful, anxious, depressed, and the list goes on and on. I had so many issues that if someone had the ability to hold a mirror to my inner man, they would run for the hills at first glance. Like many of you, I was always a good person and I had a big heart. However, the hurt, pain, and trauma of my life's experiences molded me into a person I never wanted to become.

I walked around most of my life with a constant void in my heart not being raised by my biological father. Although I was raised with a wonderful stepdad, I longed for the presence of my natural father. By the time I was an adolescent, I attempted to pursue a relationship with my dad. Unfortunately, he had no desire to pursue a relationship with me. I felt rejected and unworthy more than ever before. All the negative thoughts and feelings growing up regarding not being good enough or worthy enough was heightened. As a result, I looked to relationships with different men to fill this void. Some of these relationships turned out to be extremely toxic and resulted in physical abuse. The toxicity I carried within my soul contributed a lot to this abuse. I brought a lot of toxicity to the table. I secretly desired for the men I was in a relationship with to take on more of a "father-figure" role than a significant another role. I would feel loved and a sense of worth when they told me what to do, where to go, and how to dress. I would intentionally provoke them into a jealousy so they would react in a way that proved to me that I had self-worth and value.

These unhealthy responses by the men I was in a relationship with caused me to feel good about myself. I knew now there was a man somewhere that cared enough about me to control me, tell me what to do, and even physically fight me. By this, I felt loved and accepted as opposed to feeling rejected, which stemmed from the absence of my father. I continually attracted dysfunctional, unstable, unhealthy relationships because inside I was dysfunctional, unstable, and unhealthy. I was also incapable of being single or alone and always felt the need to be with someone in order to feel validated. As soon as one relationship ended I was instantly in another relationship with someone else. I jumped from person to person because I was unable to be by myself. I depended on other men for my happiness and fulfillment the way I depended on oxygen to breathe. Once the relationship ended, my world seemed as if it was falling apart and all my peace was lost. As a result, my mood, attention, and focus were completely altered. I would feel so nervous that I could not even eat. My emotions were up and down like a rollercoaster. As a result of my internal dysfunction, I brought a lot of grief into my parent's household. I was very rude and disrespectful. I disregarded all rules and was very disobedient. I often stayed out all night getting drunk only to return home wreaking of alcohol. I remember hanging out with friends, getting so drunk, and then jumping in the train tracks of the train station in order to urinate. I can still recall the time I attempted to take my life by drinking pills with alcohol. My life seemed to be spiraling downward. It seemed as if I was on the fast track to destruction. As if matters could not get any worse, I was sexually assaulted by a family member. I got pregnant as a result of that sexual assault. I then had an abortion. My self-worth was at an all-time low, while my shame and guilt were at an all-time high. I remember praying to God asking him to let me die because I was experiencing so much hurt and pain.

Like only I knew how to do, I continued my pursuit with relationships and other unhealthy, external outlets to fill my internal void. I got pregnant a second time from one of these relationships. I then had another abortion. A numbness began to develop on the inside of me. I was walking around numb and did not care about myself or much of anything else. At this point in my life, I had no expectations of anything positive coming from my life and I'm sure the people around me felt the same. One of my favorite things to do was to have "pity parties" for myself. This is where I would sit and think of how bad I had it and how horrible my life was. I would put on a slow love song, bury my face in my pillow, and scream and cry into it so no one would hear me. I would then look at myself crying in the mirror as to have pity on myself. I enjoyed walking around feeling sorry for myself. I wanted people to look at me, have pity on me, and feel sorry for me as well. I wanted people to notice me with a sad look on my face so they can ask me if I was ok, only for me to reply sternly, I'm fine.

My life changed once I got pregnant for the third time. I was about 21 years old, still depending on relationships to define me and bring me acceptance. Once I found out I was pregnant, I already knew like clockwork the formula to get out of the situation. I knew I would make yet another appointment at the abortion clinic and settle the matter. The numbness I carried no longer even allowed me to feel guilty about it. However, once I informed my always supportive and extremely loving mother of the situation, she spoke with me and convinced me not to go through with the procedure. As I got further along in my pregnancy, the relationship I was in with my boyfriend grew rocky and eventually ended. Like always, I was afraid to be alone and was dependent upon another person for my acceptance and happiness. You would not believe, I got into another relationship with someone else. So here I am pregnant with one guy's baby while in a relationship with another guy.

This relationship did not last long and once again, I was back to square one of being alone and feeling completely empty.

A friend of mine who knew of my current situation with being pregnant, my past hurts and struggles and mostly, my failed relationships reached out to me. She was a Christian and she began to call me on a consistent basis to check on me and encourage me. I will be honest and say that I dodged her phone calls a few times. However, this never stopped her pursuit. She consistently encouraged me and told me how much God loved me and how he had a great plan for my life. She was newly married and pregnant herself. I remember thinking that her life is in a great place so she could not possibly understand my detriment and what I'm going through. I remember thinking I could never have what she has regarding the happiness of a stable family. She continued and continued to call me regularly and have these encouraging talks with me. She eventually invited me to her church. I reluctantly went as I felt I had nothing to lose. At this time I'm about 6 months pregnant, and in a total mess internally. I'm completely broken, I'm numb and I'm lost.

When I first attended the church service, I felt so uplifted and inspired. I began to feel encouraged. I began to feel hope. They spoke of God giving me almost like a clean slate and a fresh start. I didn't understand how this could happen as I'd done so many wrong things and I always walked around feeling horrible about myself. I felt so many emotions at one time. I just wanted to cry my eyes out. I eventually continued to go back again and again. The more I went, the more I wanted to go. Every time I went it seemed as if the preacher was speaking directly to my situation. This was slowly but surely making me more stable and gave me more strength to endure my situation. I gave my heart to the Lord and accepted Jesus Christ into my life. This was the game-changer for me! I have to be honest. I cannot say that everything in my life changed overnight. But I am saying that I made a decision to stick with God long enough until I experienced a change on the inside of me. I was encouraged to go back to school as people would ask me what plan I had to support my unborn child. I decided to go to school for nursing. God gave me the grace and strength to be pregnant and go to school at the same time. He helped me to obtain straight A's and get into one of the most challenging nursing programs in NY. God completely changed my life for the better and was the game-changer in my world. I tried getting healed of many things I was going through internally. I tried to get healed through relationships, alcohol, partying, self-help classes, etc. All those things helped for a short period of time but it was like placing a band-aid on a big wound. It was only a temporary fix but I needed the wounds on the inside of me to be healed and not just covered.

I was in a fight for my life and my sanity. This time was different because I was not just fighting for myself but I was fighting for my unborn child. I was fighting for his future and a sense of normalcy and stability in his world. For the first time, I had a reason for the attention and focus to be on something other than myself and my world. I continued the pursuit of my relationship with God. I was desperate for change and desperate to be healed. Once I heard that healing and change were available to me, I wanted to stop at nothing until I received it. I made it a priority to pray daily about everything. I tried to make it to church as often as I could, sometimes twice a week. When I was home I would keep my television on Gospel channels to hear encouraging words and I would read my bible often. The more I took in God's word, whether through the preacher, my bible, or the television, the more the things I struggled with would fall off of me. It was the strangest thing! I began to grow stronger and stronger on the inside and in my faith. I birthed a beautiful son. It was not always a smooth sailing ride co-parenting. Like many other co-parenting situations, there were many arguments and disagreements. There were many childish games played and outside forces that complicated the dynamic. However, although the dynamic of my situation did not immediately change, God began to change me in the situation. God began to give me wisdom and strategies on how to handle the situation. He began to encourage me that no matter what it looked like, to not lose my peace and my joy.

Eventually, this situation no longer had a hold on me internally and emotionally. I eventually became a member of the church I was attending. I then became busy working within the church. I started volunteering to clean the church, I started ushering and helping out in any way I could. I was so grateful to God for the healing and peace that was beginning to take place in my life and I wanted to do anything for him that I possibly could. This type of serving also helped me to be more disciplined and stable minded. Mostly, it taught me to take the attention off of myself and instead to think of others. For so long my world was consumed with my hurt, my feelings, my pain, my trauma, and my emotions that it did not allow me to focus on much more of anything or anyone else. I loved this new way of living where I focused on God and helping and serving others. I discovered this was the true secret to joy and fulfillment!

As I continued to grow in my pursuit with God and developing my relationship with him, he spoke to me through my Pastor for me to take a whole season and just be single. Oh boy. Ask me for a million dollars God but don't ask me to be single! This was the main thing I always struggled with. However, looking back I can honestly say that season I took of being single was one of the greatest seasons of my life. This is when I really began to learn who I was in God and how much he truly loved me. God became so real in my world. The more I spent time with him by listening to gospel music, praying, or reading the word of God, the more peace, joy, fulfillment, and love I felt on the inside. God literally loved me back to life during this season. It's as if all the trauma, bitterness, depression, low self-worth, rejection, the hardness of heart, shame, and everything else began to fall off of me! I had such a strong focus on God, my toddler son, serving in church, my studies, and getting my degree that there wasn't much room left for anything else. I began to flourish and thrive. I felt God leading me to create a vision board of what I wanted my future to look like. I had such a bulls-eye focus like never before. Looking back at my vision board now, the majority of things I placed have come to pass!

Today I am 37 years old and I've been in a love relationship with God for 16 years. However, please keep in mind and take into account that this is 16 years of failing, making many mistakes, getting back up, failing and getting back up again and again. However, as stated earlier, I refused to give up! Today I have a Bachelor's degree in Nursing. God blessed me with a wonderful, loving husband. We just celebrated 10 years of marriage and we are still so in love! I love my husband but I am by no means dependent on him for my joy, happiness, or fulfillment. I am also blessed with 3 wonderful sons. The rocky, co-parenting relationship I had with my oldest son's father turned out to be a beautiful friendship. My son's father had another son from a different relationship. Today, I and my husband are actually the godparents to this child. God is so good! This took place after I gave the situation completely over to God. I have also been blessed to purchase a beautiful home, a few cars, and the ability to pursue my dream and passion for acting and starting a new business. I'm most blessed that he uses me consistently to help others and share my story of how he changed my life. I can honestly say my life is so blessed and full, not because of what I possess physically but what I possess spiritually. I no longer depend on people or my relationships to bring me happiness or fulfillment. Today I have so much joy, peace, and mostly LOVE. God has loved me in such a tremendous way that it forces me to love myself and others the way he loves me. I was once so critical of myself but now I love myself both inside and out. I am overflowing with so much love in my heart now that I cannot help but pour out that same love on others, even those that seem unlovable!

I tell my story of the things I went through in my past, being raped, having abortions, toxic relationships, a suicide attempt and I can honestly say when I tell my story I feel as if I'm talking about another person. I am so far removed and healed from all the hurt, trauma, and disappointment from my past. But I had to make a decision to stick with God long enough for him to do the work in me that needed to be done. I cannot stress enough that my journey was not an overnight wonder! I had to stick with it and stick with it. I made many, many mistakes even after starting my journey with God but the beautiful thing is that you don't have to be perfect in order to be in a relationship with him. In fact, I encourage you to have a real conversation with him. You can talk as real to God as you would your best friend. And if you have no desire to be in a relationship with God, tell him that and ask him to give you a desire for him. He knows exactly who, what and where you are. Many of us think we have to wait until we get all cleaned up before we come to him but he wants you exactly where you are just as you are. I prayed to him and said God I'm a mess but I need you. He took my broken pieces and my mess and he turned it into a message.

The message is that there is hope for your situation and anything you are facing! I don't care what it is or how bad it seems. Whatever you've done, been through, or are struggling with, the hope is that with God you always come out on the winning side. Even if your situation does not change, he will change you in the situation. There is a peace and joy that you can experience no matter what is taking place in your life. There is a hope that whatever dream you have in your heart and even those dreams that you've given up on, can and will come to pass with him. You're not too old and it's not too late! You don't have to settle. God wants the very best for you. You have a purpose and a destiny and there is a reason you were born and are alive today. There is an assignment only you can fulfill that no one else can. I encourage you to start this journey with God! If you've never started or if you were once on it and stopped, I encourage you to begin again. In this uncertain world, we live in today, with so much craziness going on, the only hope we have is in the one who never changes, and that is Jesus Christ.

God is my hero! He saved the day. He saved my life. The way he did it for me, I know he can and will do it for you if you just give him a try. The things I used to be so ashamed of and struggled with, I no longer struggle with those things. I used to feel so disgusting on the inside as a result of my encounter with sexual abuse. I remember my son as a toddler laying on top of me and I used to feel so uncomfortable and disgusting. I no longer struggle with those feelings. I no longer feel the feeling of shame, disgust, low self-esteem, low self-worth, or feeling like I'm not good enough. I know now that I am good enough, I am worthy of love and every good thing that God has to offer. I know that I'm chosen, I have self-worth and I have a purpose and a destiny. I know that what I've done, what happened to me, and what I struggled with does not define who I am. But my identity comes from God.

He put the broken pieces of my heart and my life back together again. But I had to make the first step in trying him out. I had to come to the end of doing things my own way and trying to figure things out on my own. I want to encourage you to do the same. If you want a different result, you have to attempt something different. You can't follow other people and what they're doing. You have to be willing to be different. Don't take advice from someone who is still struggling in their own situation. But take the advice from someone who has been where you are and came out on the winning side. I told you how my friend called me and encouraged me about how God can make all the difference in my life. I had to make the decision to take the advice, try it and stick with it long enough until I saw results. I am now encouraging you about the goodness of God and how he changed my life. Please, take my advice, try him and stick with him long enough until you see results in your own life. You may be thinking, well that worked for you but I don't think it will work for me. I cannot even begin to tell you time and time again how I've witnessed God change so many peoples' lives all around me! People that I know personally were struggling with some of the same things and some very different things. But God made all the difference and transformed their life just like he did mine.

I would be lying if I said I had all the answers or I had it all figured out regarding this journey called life. Like so many of you, I've tried to figure out so much regarding who I am, what identifies me, and where I fit in this world. Especially with the social media era that we live in today, everyone appears to compete to be seen and for their voices to be heard. It's such a freeing way to live knowing that my identity is not in how many followers I have or how many likes I obtain on a post. I have peace and joy no matter what is going on in my world. This type of freedom only comes with a consistent relationship with Jesus Christ. Not a perfect relationship with perfect performance but a consistent relationship. I still have so much to learn but one thing I do know for sure is I cannot make it on my own! I have too many flaws and imperfections to attempt to do life on my own terms. If it were up to me I would fail every time. I now depend on God like the air that I breathe and there is never any shortage with him. I used to believe that once I obtained degrees, had a wonderful marriage, obtained a great career, had a wonderful family, drove great cars and achieved my dreams and goals, that I would be satisfied and fulfilled. The strangest thing happened once I received everything I wanted and prayed for. I realized this only brought me temporary happiness and fulfillment. What I've learned is true lasting joy and fulfillment only comes from a personal relationship with Jesus Christ as well as when we help and serve others. The most fulfilled person walking around is the one that does not focus on self but lives a life to help and serve everyone else! I believe this is the reason so many people are dissatisfied in their life. Everything in our world forces us to focus on ourselves instead of others. When we get ourselves off our mind and begin to focus on others and how we can bless them, we unlock happiness, joy, and fulfillment we never knew we could experience.

While on the topic of focus. I've learned that I have to be very careful about where I place my focus and attention. Especially in the times, we are living in. There are a ton of distractions that exist in our world, more now than ever before. We are distracted by social media, the election, the health crisis in our nation and so much more. You will never get to the place in God of experiencing the true joy, freedom, and fulfillment that I speak of if you allow these distractions to consume your world. There is a way to be informed without allowing yourself to be consumed. I have learned not to allow anything to consume myself and my world more than God. The result is peace and joy. What you focus your attention on the most is what will eventually get on the inside of you. What gets on the inside of you will eventually spill out of you.

There's a wealth of wisdom and knowledge that will come to you when you begin your journey with God. So much download will come to you regarding how to navigate every aspect of your life like your family, career, children, health, etc. Above all else, you will begin to heal from everything that has held you bound and kept you captive from living and experiencing the best life you can possibly live. You will experience this new level of living not because of what's happening to you but because of what's happening on the inside of you. You will spill over with so much joy and love that you too will have to tell and share it with someone else. I encourage you to get free so you can set someone else free! My broken pieces of being raped, struggling with depression, rejection, a broken heart, abortions, a suicide attempt, guilt, shame, feelings of disgust, feeling dirty, and seeking fulfillment and validation from others were all put back together again when I started my journey with God. God took my broken pieces and made me over again. I was beyond pretty broken. I was pretty shattered and a pretty mess. But the transformation from the mess to the messenger would have never taken place had I not made the decision to take a step in a new direction.

Made in United States
North Haven, CT
11 January 2023

30921458R00065